From the Library of
Katie and Laura
Collins

Andersen Young Readers' Library

URSULA MORAY WILLIAMS

Illustrated by David McKee

Andersen Press · London

To
Jeremy John
Henry John
Peter John
and
Fiona Tait

First published in 1981 by
Andersen Press Limited
in association with
Hutchinson Limited,
3 Fitzroy Square,
London, W1

ISBN 0 905478 95 9
Printed in Great Britain

Contents

1

Jeffy and Miss Amity

Nobody, seeing Miss Amity and her little cat walking down the street to the library on a Saturday morning, would have believed that Miss Amity was a burglar.

She was so neat and tidy and old . . . so cheerful, and so polite. One imagined that she had worn that little black hat all her life, also the black knitted gloves, the dress with the lace-edged collar and the blue butterfly brooch pinned upon it, which must surely have been given to her on a birthday many years ago. Her eyes behind the old-fashioned spectacles flashed from one side of the street to the other, greeting her friends:

'Good morning Mrs Davis! Good morning Nurse Black! Good morning Mr Green! Perhaps the weather will clear up later? Now whatever will the Government think of next?'

Her shopping bag was full, like every other shopping bag, with packets of washing-powder, library books, fruit, postage stamps, and tins of cat-food for Jeffy her cat, but underneath the cat-food it was really a burglar bag, full of tools like jemmies and other house-breaking implements. Miss Amity just loved carrying them around with her.

Her little cat Jeffy had no idea of his mistress's wicked employment. He loved her very dearly and he called her Missammitty. She had adopted him when he was a kitten.

There are usually too many kittens in the world, which is very sad, but true, and Jeffy's excellent little mother, Miss Brown, was one of those cats who were always having too many kittens. Jeffy was one of them, and when she knew that she would not be able to keep him, Miss Brown picked him up and dropped him on the doorstep of the kindest old lady she knew, and that lady was Miss Amity.

Before she left him there his mother whispered into his ear all the maxims of good training she would normally have spread over the first few months of his life.

'Always be clean and tidy!' she told him, giving him a final spit and polish round the ears. 'Always be honest! Never take what does not belong to you . . . not once! . . . *not ever!* Think before you act, and wash before you think!'

Then she was gone, and Jeffy's head which had been so warm and comfortable under her licking tongue began to feel very cold indeed.

Miss Amity found him crying, and took him into her home and into her heart, just as his mother had hoped she would. She fed him and brought him up and promised him a happy home for ever and ever. Jeffy thought she was the best mistress in the world; he had no idea that she was really a burglar.

Not until one night when he caught her climbing in through the window, in disguise.

2

A Shock for Jeffy

Jeffy woke up with a start in the darkness. He slept inside a cupboard, curled up in Miss Amity's work-basket, and usually she shut the cupboard door when she went upstairs.

But on this particular night the cupboard door was open, just a crack, and the noise that woke Jeffy was the burglar bag being dropped on the floor as Miss Amity climbed in through the kitchen window.

Jeffy sat bolt upright in the workbasket. He was pricked by a couple of pins, so he jumped lightly on to the floor inside the cupboard.

'Miss Amity! Is that you, Miss Amity?' he called out in the darkness. Instantly there was perfect silence.

Jeffy listened, and while he listened he washed, to fill in time, and while he washed he heard somebody moving very quietly across the kitchen floor.

Quick as a flash Jeffy was round the corner of the door, and there, crawling across the linoleum, which was clearly lit up by the lamps in the street outside, was a burglar!

The burglar wore a black slouch hat and dark spectacles. He had long black moustaches dripping down his chin, and he carried a burglar bag.

Jeffy let out a screech for his mistress that must have woken all the cats in the street and some of their owners as well.

'Missammitty! Oh Missammitty! Come quickly!' He was about to follow it with: 'Thieves! Robbers! Burglars! Police! Police! Police!' when the burglar leapt to his feet and banged the window shut.

'You stupid cat! Don't you know me?' scolded the burglar, tearing off the cap, the glasses and the moustache, and there *was* Miss Amity!

Jeffy was so upset that she had to take off all the rest of her burglar clothes and make a cup of tea, so that he could have some condensed milk to settle him down.

'Well now, Jeffy!' she said when he had stopped shaking. 'What's wrong with my being a burglar, anyhow?'

'What's inside the bag?' Jeffy faltered, with spatters of condensed milk trembling on his chin.

'Nothing much!' said Miss Amity lightly.

'Really nothing much? Really *nothing?* Or how much?' Jeffy demanded.

'*Nothing* much!' said Miss Amity firmly.

'But how *much* nothing much?' Jeffy persisted.

'Oh well, just one tiny little diamond ring!' said Miss Amity defiantly.

Jeffy pounced on the bag, and drew out the ring with his paw. It was quite true; it was the only object inside the bag except the burgling tools.

'From the Towers,' said Miss Amity with satisfaction. 'She's got lots and lots more like it, and it was such lovely fun climbing up the drainpipe!'

'It's *thieving!*' said Jeffy, horrified. 'It's wicked! It's awful! I just don't know what my mother would say if she knew I'd come to live with a person that stole things.'

Miss Amity stared.

'Do you mean you think it's wrong of me, Jeffy?' she said.

'Of course it's wrong,' said Jeffy. 'My mother told me: Never never take anything that doesn't belong to you. Not once. Not ever. I just can't go on living with a person like that. My mother wouldn't like it at all.'

'Oh Jeffy dear, I'll put it back! I'll put it back!' Miss Amity said. 'I only did it for fun! I didn't mean to keep it!'

'*When* will you put it back?' Jeffy asked.

'This very minute,' said Miss Amity brightly, beginning to put on her disguise again, and snatching the ring out of Jeffy's paw.

But already the early morning was breaking on the world outside. Whistles were shrilling, and police cars came dashing up the street on their way to the Towers.

'There!' Jeffy said. 'It's no good. They've found out everything already. You can't go back now or you'll be caught.' Immediately he found he wanted to protect Miss Amity.

'Never mind,' she said bravely. 'I'll face them. I'll tell the truth. I'll explain I only did it for fun. I'll say it was just a game and I was going to put it back the next morning.'

'You burgled,' said Jeffy. 'They'll punish you just the same.'

'But surely not if I say I'm sorry?' said Miss Amity, crestfallen. '*You* believe me, don't you, Jeffy?'

'I'm not a policeman,' said Jeffy. 'So I think the best thing to do is to put it back myself.'

'Oh what a *good* idea! What a clever little cat you are!' said Miss Amity. 'Would you like to borrow my whiskers and my cap and my gloves and my burglar bag? They may be a little big for you, my dear!'

'I don't want any of them,' said Jeffy severely. 'Just give me the ring.'

'Oh well,' said Miss Amity, 'I'll have some warm milk ready for you when you come in.'

It was almost too simple, and afterwards Jeffy wished he could have had more of a narrow escape to describe to Miss Amity as a warning, when it was all over.

For there was nobody in the streets, and the driveway of the Towers was floodlit by the beams from police cars. Inside the house he could see lights blazing, and more policemen gathered round the library table, taking notes. The front door was guarded by a huge policeman standing at attention.

Jeffy just went up to him and yowled and yowled round his legs, till the policeman took pity on him, opened the door, and let him inside.

'Poor old pusskins! Did she get shut out then?

Well, well, that's what you get for going out on the tiles. Serves you right, Puss! Serves you right!'

Jeffy trotted across the empty hall to the staircase and spat the ring into a corner of the stairs. Then he went to the back of the house and yowled and yowled until another policeman let him out again.

'Poor old pussycat! Got a rendezvous? Mustn't keep Miss Tabitha waiting!'

He was back in his own house in ten minutes' time. Miss Amity had not even begun to warm the milk.

'Well,' she said, placidly filling the saucepan. 'There's nothing to it, is there?' and even as she spoke the police cars began to come back down the street, quite quietly, in the direction of the police station. It was obvious that the diamond ring had been found very quickly and everyone thought it had all been a false alarm.

But Jeffy refused to drink any milk, and went to bed in a temper. He would hardly speak to Miss Amity in the morning.

'Jeffy, Jeffy! How can you be so unkind to your missis?' Miss Amity coaxed him, nearly in tears.

'You're a burglar,' said Jeffy flatly. 'And my mother said ....'

'Oh I know, I know. But I *was* a burglar. I'm not now!' said Miss Amity happily. 'And you are a very clever, well-brought-up little cat. Your mother would be proud of you. Just think, Jeffy, I might be eating my cornflakes in prison this morning if it wasn't for you.'

'Yes,' agreed Jeffy, drinking his milk at last.

'So we'll just forget all about it, shall we, Jeffy?' coaxed Miss Amity. 'And we'll be best friends again, and go down to the grocer to fetch some tins of Catsprat. I know you like Catsprat, Jeffy. Catsprat's for clever cats!'

Jeffy could not keep up his ill-temper for long, and he was flattered by Miss Amity's praise. He hoped she had learnt her lesson, for he had had a nasty shock.

He tried to prop open the cupboard door, just a chink, at night, but Miss Amity always closed it firmly when she went to bed. Then he took to sleeping in the burglar bag. When Miss Amity tried to remove him to put him in the cupboard he clung on tightly, dragging up all the burglar things from the bottom, so that the false beard dangled from his feet and the cap fell out on to the carpet.

'Look what you've done!' Miss Amity scolded, picking them up. 'And I might never have thought of them again if you hadn't reminded me!'

Jeffy felt as guilty as if he had personally led her into temptation. But all he said was: 'You'd better not!'

3

The Mayor's Party

There were festivities in the town when the new Mayor was elected. There was to be a grand tea for the schoolchildren, and another for the Town Council, when the old Mayor would hand over his chain of office to the new one.

Jeffy and Miss Amity watched the preparations going on outside the Town Hall when they changed their books at the library. A big marquee had been put up in the public gardens, and long trestle tables were set up in it for the schoolchildren, with a big table at the end for the Mayor and Town Council to sit at.

On the morning of the party Miss Amity said she would just slip out to the shops to get a little bit of fish for their dinner, and afterwards she would take Jeffy to see the procession that would go through the town before the Mayor was elected and everybody went in to tea.

Jeffy was sitting on the window-sill in the sunshine when Miss Amity returned. She came flying down the street, and indeed she was puffing as if she had done quite a lot of running. The shopping bag, when she put it down, sounded heavy.

There was something much heavier than fish in Miss Amity's shopping bag.

'What have you got in that bag, Missammitty?' said Jeffy suspiciously.

'Nothing!' said Miss Amity with spirit.

'Do you mean nothing? Or nothing to do with me?' asked Jeffy.

'Nothing to do with you!' snapped Miss Amity.

'Ha!' said Jeffy. 'And perhaps that means nothing to do with you either! Am I right, Missammitty?'

'Oh well, if you put it that way . . . yes!' said Miss Amity looking coy, and giggling a little.

'Have you been burgling again?' Jeffy asked her.

'Why no, Jeffy, no! Of course I wouldn't! Burgling is done at night in burglar's clothes with jemmies and things. Do I look as if I had been burgling?' said Miss Amity with indignation.

'Well, stealing, then! Robbery! Daylight robbery?' suggested Jeffy.

Miss Amity cast down her eyes and tried to shuffle the shopping bag behind her skirts. 'Well, just a little bit,' she admitted.

Jeffy lost his temper with her.

'This time it's too much! I'm going to leave you!' he expostulated.

'Oh Jeffy, Jeffy!' Miss Amity cried, taking off her gloves and flinging them on to the floor. 'I didn't mean it! I didn't mean it! I didn't really! I do want to be honest and live a good life like your mother told you to do! Oh what shall I do? What shall I do?'

'What did you take this time?' Jeffy asked crossly.

'Not much,' said Miss Amity slyly, still trying to keep the bag from Jeffy's view.

'Well, what?'

'Only two little sandwiches!'

'And?'

'And two tomatoes ....'

'And ....'

'And some mustard'n cress ....'

'AND ...?'

'And the Mayor's chain of office!' wept Miss Amity, bursting into tears and hurling a handful of golden metal across the room with such force that it cracked the sink.

'Now look what you've done,' cried Jeffy. 'When we wash up all the water will go on the floor. Oh why, why, why do you do such things, Missammitty?'

'I don't know,' wept Miss Amity. 'I didn't mean to throw it so hard. I didn't mean it!'

'Not the sink ... *the Mayor's chain of office*!' said Jeffy. 'And the sandwiches and the tomatoes and the mustard and cress! It's all of it pinching and stealing and wickedness, and I've told you before my mother said I wasn't to have anything to do with it. I'm off!'

'Oh, Jeffy! Jeffy!' wept Miss Amity, collapsing on top of the sandwiches with her head on her arms.

'Don't do that! You're squashing them!' Jeffy cried in alarm. 'And then we won't be able to take them back.'

'Oh will you really, dear Jeffy? Oh Jeffy, how good you are to poor, wicked old me!' Miss Amity cried, getting up and prancing for joy. 'Then I won't have to go to prison, and we'll live happily ever after! Oh you are the very best little cat in all the world, and I don't deserve you, I know I don't!'

'I may not come back to you afterwards,' Jeffy said severely, sweeping the sandwiches, the tomatoes and the mustard and cress into a paper bag, and winding the Mayor's chain several times round his neck under the thick fur of his collar and chin. 'My mother would have a fit if she knew I was living with a thief and a robber, and I don't like it myself one little bit.'

'Don't you love me any more?' said Miss Amity, with tears now running down her chin. 'Your mother was quite right. I don't deserve to have a cat like you, and I must do without it. But I shall think of you all the rest of my life. Promise me just one thing before you leave me for ever. When you have taken back the sandwiches, Jeffy dear, and the tomatoes, and the mustard and cress and the Mayor's golden chain, come back and show yourself to me for just one little minute, so that I can be sure that they haven't caught you and put you in prison!'

'Pah!' said Jeffy crossly. But to set her mind at rest he promised Miss Amity that he would.

Nobody took much notice of a little cat trotting through the streets with a paper bag in its mouth. They thought it had been stealing out of dustbins.

Jeffy could not run fast, because the weight of the chain wound round his neck was quite suffocating, and he found it difficult to raise his head.

Outside the Town Hall a queue of schoolchildren was impatiently waiting to go into the marquee where tea was set out on long tables, but inside, everyone was frantically searching for the chain of office, which seemed to have completely disappeared. They were so busy that it was easy enough for Jeffy to jump on to the table and replace the sandwiches, the tomatoes and the mustard and cress, but the heavy chain so weighed him down that he landed with a crash among the crockery, which brought the waitresses running into the tent, joined by half a dozen waiters from the kitchen.

'Cat's after the food!' they shouted, and Jeffy was chased from one end of the table to the other, dodging glasses, plates and bowls of jelly as he ran, until, in making a great leap to escape from his pursuers he fell with a splash into an enormous bowl of fruit salad that the Mayor had specially ordered to please the children.

The caterers, the waitresses and the waiters all sprang backwards to escape the fountains of juice cascading over the table. Then they fled to the kitchen to find cloths to wipe up the mess, while Jeffy clawed for the edge of the bowl.

As he did so, the golden chain of office slipped off his wet and slippery neck into the bottom of the salad. The chief of the caterers found it there later when he emptied out the bowl in the kitchen, to replace it with

fresh fruit. He thought somebody must have been playing tricks on him.

'And if it hadn't been for that perishing cat we might never have found it!' he said, carrying the chain in triumph to the Mayor.

Jeffy arrived home sticky with fruit juice and with apricot slices clinging to his fur.

Miss Amity bathed and dried him, telling him how good and clever he was.

'It's all very well,' Jeffy said, giving his coat an angry licking after the bath, 'but if I hadn't fallen into the fruit salad they would have caught me, and I would have been put into prison instead of you. Just because you went out stealing like a common thief.'

'But I'll never do it again, dear Jeffy,' Miss Amity promised, drying him with tender hands. 'Not if you will stay with me and make sure that I don't, and keep reminding me what your good little mother taught you.'

'Will you *promise*?' said Jeffy, feeling warm and comfortable again.

'I promise I will never be a common thief again,' said Miss Amity.

'Or a burglar,' Jeffy insisted.

'Or a burglar,' Miss Amity promised. 'Never again! Not ever!'

4

In the Woods

The next day, in front of Jeffy, she burned up the burglar bag, and the cap and the beard, and put the burgling tools into the dustbin. Jeffy saw the dustmen take them away, and all at once he felt much safer.

But Miss Amity complained that now her bag was gone she had nothing to put her shopping or her library books in, and she did not like the plastic bags they gave her in the shops, so she bought a brown, canvas haversack that she could sling over her shoulder.

'It doesn't look ladylike,' Jeffy objected.

'But it is so useful, Jeffy,' said Miss Amity. 'And what is more, I can ride you down town in it.'

Jeffy did not criticise the haversack after that, because he often grew footsore on the pavements, and he only went into town with Miss Amity in order to look after her. It was quite a relief to ride down in the haversack.

Then Miss Amity bought a new hat. It was not a bit like the burglar cap, but it was not at all like Miss Amity either. It was made of fur and turned down all round, with a peak, and ear flaps.

'I don't like it a bit,' said Jeffy. 'What do you want to buy a hat like that for? It looks like a fur trapper's hat, not a lady's!'

'Oh Jeffy, don't be so stuffy and dull!' said Miss

Amity. 'I'm tired of my old black hat and my old black gloves and my old black coat. I never wear anything else. Why shouldn't I have something different for a change?'

'Well it will look very odd with your black dress and your butterfly brooch,' said Jeffy, so the next day Miss Amity bought a moleskin jacket and a bright red handkerchief to tie round her neck, with white spots on it. She also bought some string, and said she was going to do some handwork for the Church Bazaar.

'Well don't ask me to go down town with you, dressed up like that,' said Jeffy, but Miss Amity only laughed at him. She kept her new clothes hanging in her cupboard, and threatened every day to put them on.

One morning Jeffy awoke to a strange noise going on in the kitchen. He had gone back to sleeping in the workbox, thinking all his worries were over, so he slept very soundly indeed.

The noise was not exactly footsteps, and yet it was the sound of feet. Somebody or something was running round and round and round the kitchen, and when Jeffy jumped out of the cupboard (he had not been shut in for weeks now) he found a full-grown rabbit rushing round the kitchen floor.

And there was more to it than that. Miss Amity's furry hat was perched on the table, covered with grass and leaves. Her moleskin jacket hung on a chair, and it had certainly been torn by brambles. Her red handkerchief had fallen to the floor beside the open haversack, from which protruded a jumble of string that was certainly not a piece of handwork for the Church Bazaar. It looked much more like a rabbit snare.

When the rabbit saw Jeffy it bolted behind the coalscuttle, but Jeffy ignored it, and went straight through the kitchen to Miss Amity's bedroom. She was lying on her back snoring, and very sound asleep indeed.

Jeffy just jumped on to the bed and pounded with his feet upon her chest until she woke up.

'Missammitty!' he hissed, right in her face. 'You've been poaching and I've had enough of it and I'm off!'

'Oh no, Jeffy!' Miss Amity shrieked, sitting bolt upright, and then she added: 'You've been dreaming!'

'There's a full-grown rabbit running round our kitchen,' said Jeffy. 'And so far as I can see it got out of a bag. And the bag was your bag! And it had a rabbit snare inside it!'

'Oh Jeffy,' Miss Amity wheedled, her eyes sparkling with excitement. 'It was such fun, Jeffy, such fun! I wanted you to come with me, but I thought you would be cross.'

'My mother told me . . .' Jeffy began, but Miss Amity interrupted him quite rudely. 'Oh bother your mother!' she exclaimed. 'Think of rabbit pie, Jeffy . . . lovely tasty rabbit pie!'

Jeffy's mouth watered at the thought of it, but he jumped lightly off the bed. He was angry at the insult to his mother.

'Eat your rabbit pie!' he said, thrashing his tail. 'And much good may it do you. Just wait till they smell it down at the police station along the road. You know what the law is about poaching on other people's property. I shouldn't wonder if you didn't get seven years! I hope you enjoy your pie first! I shan't be here to see it. I'm nearly gone already.'

'Oh no, Jeffy, don't leave me!' Miss Amity wailed. 'We've been so happy together since I was honest again. I can't bear to think of what my life will be without you. What's one little rabbit between us, Jeffy? One little pie? I only did it for fun, Jeffy. I wanted to know what it felt like to be a poacher!'

'Well now you know,' said Jeffy. 'And I hope you like it!'

'I don't much,' Miss Amity admitted. 'It was dark and lonely out in the woods and I got horribly scratched by brambles. Night birds made dreadful noises at me. I'll never, never do it again! Will you stay with me, Jeffy, if I put the rabbit back and give all my poaching clothes to the Jumble Sale?'

Jeffy washed himself all over before he replied.

'What about the snare?' he asked.

'I'll turn it into a macramé bag for the Bazaar,' she told him brightly.

'All right,' he agreed at last, very unwillingly.

Miss Amity dressed and went into the kitchen to catch the rabbit.

The upheaval that followed was disastrous. Miss Amity pursued, the rabbit escaped. Tables and chairs were upset, crockery clattered to the floor. It was worse than the chase at the Mayor's party, and the neighbours in the houses on either side of Miss Amity's began knocking on the wall.

Jeffy had been watching her efforts with the utmost scorn. When Miss Amity was quite exhausted and helpless he made a quiet pounce, and caught the rabbit with no effort at all. He held it gently dangling from his mouth. 'Never mind, little bunny,' he murmured. 'You'll soon be home.'

Miss Amity was now in tears.

'Do take it back for me, Jeffy, please do,' she pleaded. 'I've had such an exhausting night, and I know it will escape again if I try.'

Jeffy said nothing. He merely trotted out of the back door, up the garden path to the fence, and took the shortest route to the woods. Nobody took much notice of him. One or two dogs and cats eyed him for a moment or turned in their tracks, but the glint in his eye was enough to persuade them to mind their own business.

Jeffy trotted as far as the edge of the wood, and was about to let the rabbit go when a fox went by. Jeffy knew that foxes sometimes liked a juicy rabbit for their suppers, and this rabbit was tired and frightened. He didn't want to carry it all this way just to let it fall into the jaws of a hungry fox, or to be taken home to its cubs.

So he waited until the fox had passed by, and then dived deeper into the wood among the bracken and the blackberries, in case it should come back again.

At last he stopped and released the rabbit, who bounded away without a hint of gratitude. Jeffy watched it go, and was just turning towards home, when an enormous bang! and explosion sent him head-over-heels backwards into the undergrowth.

Jeffy was not hurt, but he was stunned by the shot from the keeper's gun, and he lay barely conscious in the bracken. The keeper had no difficulty at all in finding him and picking him up in a couple of minutes.

'Ha, ha, my beauty! All right, my handsome, don't scratch! Peter the Poacher . . . eh? Thieving Thomas! How will you like to join the band of robbers hanging on my cottage wall?' the keeper said, thrusting Jeffy into his bag. Jeffy kicked and struggled in vain.

The keeper trudged home with him through the woods, whistling.

'Have you got a rabbit in the bag, Dad?' his children asked.

'Not likely!'

'A squirrel?'

'No.'

'A bird?'

'No, it isn't a bird.'

'Well, what is it, Dad? It's kicking! Do tell us, Dad!'

'It's a thieving, poaching, sneaking old tomcat that's come into the woods to steal my baby pheasants,' said the keeper in triumph. When he was sure that all the doors and windows were shut he tipped Jeffy out of his satchel on to the kitchen floor.

'Oh it's a *beautiful* cat,' said the keeper's children in delight.

'Ha!' said the keeper. 'That's all *you* know!'

'What are you going to do with it?' they asked him anxiously.

'What do I do with my other thieves that take my baby pheasants?' said the keeper. 'What do I do with the jays? What do I do with the crows? What do I do with the stoatses and the weasels and the ratses and the hawks? Bang! Bang! And string up the corpses along the wall, to warn other poachers to keep away!'

'Oh no, no, no, Dad! You mustn't shoot the lovely pussycat,' the children pleaded, and they made such a commotion that the keeper decided he would put Jeffy in the old ferret cage on the wall, instead, so the other raiders would see him and stay clear of the young pheasants.

The cage smelt very unpleasant indeed to Jeffy, who had never had anything to do with ferrets. The keeper told the children they were not to let the cat out or they'd wish they had never been born.

The children gave Jeffy a saucer of milk and some meat and potatoes, but they dared not let him escape, for fear of their father.

All day long Jeffy sat in the cage, looking out on to the keeper's string of dead jays, weasels, stoats and other vermin. It was terribly humiliating for him, and he had never been enclosed in quite so small a space as this before. Even the cupboard was much bigger than this. He did not blame Miss Amity for what had happened to him, but he longed for her with all his heart and soul, and wondered who would take care of her now that he was not there to keep her out of mischief.

The sun went down. The children went indoors to bed, and a great moon crept slowly up the sky. Jeffy sat sadly in the ferret's cage, thinking over all the happy years he had spent with Miss Amity, and wondering what he might have done to keep her from getting into so much trouble. He wished he could have gone to his mother for advice, but a cat ought to be able to shape his own life by now.

In spite of the confined space he washed himself so many times that he felt quite invisible, but no ideas came to him that might have improved the past nor mended the present, and after a while Jeffy slept.

All of a sudden he woke with all his senses alive and twitching. For a moment he thought he was in the cupboard at home, and his first thought was 'Missammitty! What is happening to Missammitty?' But then he saw the trees swaying gently in the night breeze around the keeper's cottage, and the moon hanging like a great white eye in the deep blue darkness of the night.

The keeper's dogs were not barking. What could have awakened him? Jeffy stared ahead at the moonlit space in front of the cottage, and saw that something was creeping across it.

Jeffy stiffened, and stared. Was it a dog? Or a fox? Or a badger? What midnight creature was approaching carefully on four legs and making no sound at all?

The creature was furry. It had a furry head, furry ears that hung down on either side of its face, and a kind of beak. But no, it was not really a beak, for that was furry too. And the front paws advancing so carefully were more like arms, only they were covered in a close kind of fur. As it came nearer and nearer Jeffy saw it was no beast of the night, but Miss Amity, wearing her furry hat and her moleskin jacket. And for the life of him he could not prevent himself from uttering a joyful mew, if only to show Miss Amity that he had seen her, and to show her where he was imprisoned.

Immediately one of the keeper's dogs barked. Miss Amity lay flat on the ground. Then a window opened and the keeper's head poked out. All the dogs in their kennels began to bark at once.

'Aha,' came the keeper's voice above the noise that

they were making. 'I see you! A fox this time, I think. I'll get you, Mr Reynard! Just wait while I fetch my gun.'

Jeffy heard him running down the stairs.

'Missammitty! Missammitty!' he cried, and Miss Amity sprang upright from her four paws and rushed to his cage. Her black knitted gloves seized hold of the bolt and wrenched at it. The door came open. Jeffy leapt out. Side by side they fled across the open space and into the woods. When they had run a short distance there was an enormous bang! behind them, and some stray shot pattered harmlessly into the branches above their heads. But by now they were well out of sight of the keeper and running hard. They heard no further shots, and reached home breathless at about one o'clock in the morning.

Miss Amity hugged Jeffy to her bosom as if she would never let him go, but her eyes were sparkling.

'Now don't tell me you enjoyed all that,' said Jeffy anxiously, for although he was deeply grateful to her, he did not like her triumphant manner at all.

'No, of course not, dear, true, faithful little Jeffy! I hated every minute, but it was rather an exciting adventure all the same, wasn't it?' said Miss Amity.

'It may have been exciting for you, but what about me?' said Jeffy. 'It was no thanks to you, Misssammitty, that I wasn't shot dead by the keeper long before you came. It was only the children crying that saved me. What would you have said then?'

'I would never, never have forgiven myself, however long I lived,' said Miss Amity solemnly, and in front of his eyes she stuffed the fur cap, the moleskin jacket, the haversack and the red neckerchief into the kitchen stove. The burning fur made the most appalling smell, worse than the ferret's cage, but Jeffy would not allow her to pull it out again. He made her sit and smell it till it was gone.

5

Little Lew

Miss Amity was very quiet for a great many weeks after this incident. True to her word she unravelled the rabbit snare, and knitted it into a bag, but she did not give it to the Church Bazaar. She kept it for her shopping.

Jeffy became uneasy about her, she seemed so listless and depressed. She went off her food and seemed to find little pleasure in her library books, but then Jeffy would not let her borrow any stories about crime or detectives, which were the books she loved best. He persuaded her to go for walks past the Magistrates' Court and the local prison, to remind her where she might end up if she wasn't careful, and to show her that Crime Doesn't Pay.

He was very pleased when Miss Amity agreed that she could not imagine anything worse than to be shut up in a little cell, and never to be able to go and have a cup of coffee in town, or to take tea with her friends. Never, never, never, she told Jeffy, would she run the risk of being shut up inside such a place. Jeffy would have felt quite encouraged about her if Miss Amity had not gradually become so miserable that he felt he might have overdone her reformation.

But fortunately something happened to restore her spirits, and within a few days she had something to think about that brought back all her old vitality and good humour.

She found another kitten on the doorstep.

To tell the truth it was Jeffy who found it first . . . a little black scrap of a kitten with its eyes hardly open, big, splattered paws, a short triangle of a tail, and a small, pink, innocent nose. He went to tell Miss Amity.

'Stray cat at the door, Missammitty,' he reported.

Miss Amity had no intention of adopting another cat. It would not have come into her head. But when she removed the kitten from the steps to the pavement it climbed back again, and went on doing it however many times she put it into the street.

'Do you think we ought to keep it, Jeffy?' she asked him.

Jeffy could never forget that Miss Amity had taken him in and given him a home at much the same stage of helplessness, and he could not bear the thought of shutting the door on the little creature.

'Well, I don't mind if you don't,' he told Miss Amity.

They took in the kitten and gave it a home.

Quite soon it became apparent that it was quite a different kind of cat from Jeffy. It was not a little girl cat, as Miss Amity had secretly hoped, but a romping, randy little tom kitten.

It was, in fact, a handful.

When it arrived it was only just old enough to tell them that its name was Little Lew. And it had not the

slightest idea where it came from, but thought it might have been down by the docks, because it could just remember the clanking of chains and the shouts of sailors.

As it grew older it admired and hero-worshipped Jeffy, following him everywhere. It said: 'Yes, Jeffy!' and 'No, Jeffy!' and for a while obeyed him in everything he told it to do.

It also said: 'Yes, Missammitty! No, Missammitty!' but Miss Amity indulged it shockingly, and the kitten took every advantage. Jeffy warned her that kittens should be spanked when they did wrong, and one could not begin too early to teach them good behaviour, but Miss Amity laughed so much at Little Lew's naughtiness and the tricks he got up to, that Jeffy consoled himself by thinking that at least she had cheered up and left her depression behind her.

He was very fond of Little Lew himself, even when the kitten became cheeky and impertinent. As often as he was able to he repeated to it the lessons learned and remembered from his mother's teaching:

'Be clean and tidy, Lew! Always be honest. Never take what does not belong to you . . . not once, not ever! Think before you act, and wash before you think!'

'Yes, Jeffy. No, Jeffy. Yes I will, Jeffy,' said Little Lew, but he only washed when Jeffy was looking at him, and he often snicked a bit of fish out of the frying pan. Jeffy knew he did, because the fish was hot, and he found Little Lew crying with a burnt mouth beside the kitchen stove.

'That'll teach him,' said Miss Amity, but it did not. The next day Jeffy found that Little Lew had put a piece of fish on the window-sill to cool. Jeffy spanked him with a hard paw, and Little Lew ran yelling to Miss Amity, who told Jeffy he was cruel.

'I only want to teach him to be honest,' said Jeffy, hurt.

'There are better ways of teaching him than that,' said Miss Amity, and she took Little Lew for walks beside the prison to show him what happened to people who stole and were dishonest.

But Jeffy wished that she would not tell Little Lew stories of the days when she was a burglar and stole the diamond ring, and how Jeffy had put it back again. Little Lew listened, his eyes round with delight, gazing first at Miss Amity and then at Jeffy.

'So you see, Jeffy is the best and kindest and the bravest cat that ever was,' Miss Amity finished up. 'He is an example to us all.'

'I mean to grow up just like Jeffy,' said Little Lew.

The next day he wanted more stories, and Miss Amity told him about the Mayor's tea-party, and how she had stolen the Mayor's chain of office. Little Lew rolled on the floor, squealing with excitement and delight.

'If only I could have been with you, Missammitty!' he cried. 'I could have carried the mustard'n cress all by myself!' He mewed with joy. Miss Amity smiled to see him.

'No!' exclaimed Jeffy, very crossly. 'I don't think you ought to tell him such things, Missammitty. I don't really! It won't do him any good.'

'Ah, but it isn't the end of the story,' said Miss Amity wisely, and she told Little Lew how Jeffy had taken back the sandwiches and the tomatoes and the mustard and cress and the Mayor's chain of office, and had nearly been caught while he was putting them back where they came from.

'And did Jeffy really fall into the fruit salad?' cried Little Lew. 'Oh my! Oh my! I do wish I had been there to see Jeffy falling into the bowl of fruit salad!'

Miss Amity laughed too. Jeffy was very annoyed, and went out into the street. When he came back again Miss Amity was scolding Little Lew and telling him what a hero Jeffy really was.

'But if you hadn't taken away the Mayor's chain first, Jeffy couldn't have fallen into the fruit salad and been a hero, could he, Missammitty?' said Little Lew.

'I don't like to hear you talk like that, Lewie,' said Miss Amity gravely. 'I hope you are going to grow up into a fine honest cat like Jeffy!'

'Oh yes, Missammitty, I will,' said Little Lew.

But before long she was telling him the story of her poaching expedition, and Little Lew seemed to find exquisite pleasure in picturing the rabbit hopping about the kitchen in the middle of the night.

'But poor Jeffy was shut up in a horrid old ferret's cage for nearly a whole day and a night,' Miss Amity reminded him. 'It was I who rescued him this time.'

'Then I'd like to grow up just like you, Missammitty,' said Little Lew.

'You're much more likely to end up in a cage yourself, if you go on at this rate,' said Jeffy severely. 'You don't know what it's like. Bars in front of you, bars behind you. There you are . . . stuck, till somebody lets you out. Sometimes the wrong ones get shut up, you know. That's what comes of other people being wicked.'

'I know, Jeffy dear, and I've told him all about it. We walk past the prison every day,' Miss Amity said. Little Lew suddenly gave a squeal of laughter and tore round the kitchen.

'Can't catch me and shut me up,' he yelled. 'I'm an escaped prisoner! Catch me, Jeffy, catch me!'

But Jeffy refused to play, and looked at him with disapproval. He thought Little Lew was getting too big for his boots.

And although he had no doubt of Miss Amity's gratitude and her deep affection for him, he could not prevent the odd spark of jealousy when he saw how very close the pair of them had become. Miss Amity and Little Lew were seldom apart these days; they often seemed to be sharing secret jokes in which Jeffy had no part at all.

When he asked what they were laughing at, Miss

Amity would just turn it aside.

'Oh we are just being silly, Jeffy,' she would say. 'Little Lew is such a baby! It really isn't anything funny at all.'

Jeffy still slept in the workbasket, and the kitten had a bed in a cardboard box on the floor. One day Jeffy saw that the box was lined with a beautiful yellow silk handkerchief.

'Wherever did that come from?' Jeffy asked Little Lew, staring.

Little Lew went on turning round and round on top of the handkerchief to make himself a comfortable nest.

'I was speaking to you!' said Jeffy.

'Missammitty said I wasn't to talk to you about it,' muttered Little Lew.

Jeffy waited until they were all sitting round the fire that evening with the lamp turned low.

'Well now, nobody could be so comfortable and happy as we are, could they?' said Miss Amity, warming her toes at the fire.

'Where did that yellow silk handkerchief come from in Little Lew's basket?' asked Jeffy ominously.

'Oh Jeffy, how tiresome you are! What do you want to spoil things for?' said Miss Amity peevishly.

'Where did it come from?' repeated Jeffy.

Miss Amity looked sulky, but Jeffy repeated his question, while the kitten looked from one to the other with round, bright, inquisitive eyes.

'Where did you get that handkerchief from?' Jeffy said for the fourth time, with a warning note in his voice.

'Oh well – better ask Lew,' said Miss Amity carelessly, beginning to knit.

'I got it off the street,' said the kitten, beginning to babble. 'Missammitty and I was out shopping and there was lots of people . . . lots and lots. Missammitty said, "What a chance for pickpockets!" and I said, "Oh yes, oh yes," and Missammitty said, "I wonder if it's as easy as they say?" and I said, "Oh yes I bet it is! Let's try it, Missammitty!" But Missammitty didn't do nothing about it, it was me. I just got underneath a man's feet and tripped him up and he fell over and the hanky fell out and I picked it up and we went home.'

'Why didn't you give him back the handkerchief?' said Jeffy in a fury, holding Little Lew down with one paw.

'Because it wouldn't have been pick-pocketing then,' wept Little Lew. 'And Miss Amity and me wanted to see how easy it was.'

Jeffy just looked at Miss Amity, but the blazing of his eyes quite terrified her.

'Why didn't *you* give it back to its owner?' he growled, still holding Little Lew, who was now sobbing bitterly.

'Why! The man had gone by then!' Miss Amity exclaimed. 'Somebody helped him to his feet, and there were so many people he just disappeared. It seemed a pity to *waste* the handkerchief.'

Jeffy was so angry he could not speak, and he hardly slept a wink all night. He made Little Lew sleep on the bare boards as a punishment, and in the morning he marched out of the house carrying the handkerchief, without saying goodbye to either of them.

Miss Amity and Little Lew were quite convinced he was going to leave them for ever. They cried and pleaded with him, imploring him to stay. Jeffy paid no attention to them at all.

He did not even look back as he trotted down the street to the police station, and gave the yellow silk handkerchief to the Chief Inspector.

'Well now,' said the Inspector in delight, 'there was somebody in here yesterday asking if a yellow silk handkerchief had been handed in. That's what gives the police force a good name! Splendid cat! Hundred per cent cat! Whoever heard of a cat picking up something, like a dog, and bringing it to the right place! That's a cat worth knowing, that is!'

He offered Jeffy some condensed milk and half a kipper, but Jeffy refused them both politely.

He left the police station with a heavy heart, and spent the whole day wandering about the back streets, worrying about what was to become of Miss Amity and Little Lew. He knew they were bound to get into more trouble sooner or later, without him, but he flinched at the idea of spending the rest of his life with criminals. Perhaps there was still a chance for the kitten, if he could exert a strong enough influence over him, but Miss Amity! Oh dear, Miss Amity!

It was a long, unhappy day. At one moment Jeffy decided to go far, far away and try his luck all alone, but at the next he felt he could not bear to leave them.

At last he made up his mind to go for good. He was not afraid of looking after himself, and it would be better, he decided, to go a long, long way off where he would never have to see Miss Amity or Little Lew again.

He did not believe they would really miss him. Even now they might be planning some dreadful new adventure that would give Miss Amity all the excitement she wanted, and Little Lew would be her willing accomplice.

Before leaving the district for good, Jeffy could not resist trotting back to the street where almost the whole of his life had been spent, to have one final look at the little house where he had been so happy.

It was growing dark, so he fully expected the door to be shut and the curtains drawn across the windows, but they were not. Instead, the street lamps shone upon the open workbasket, lying on the doorstep and propping open the door, while inside the basket, resting against the door jamb, was a piece of white cardboard with Miss Amity's writing on it.

The writing said: 'JEFFY COME HOME!'

Jeffy did not go straight in through the door.

He jumped lightly onto the window-sill, and peeped in through the panes.

The lamp was not yet lighted . . . the only illumination came from the fire in the grate and from the street lamps outside. Miss Amity and Little Lew had their heads bowed, and he could see the tears glistening on the kitten's shirt front, and on Miss Amity's lace collar. Now and again a big sob shook first one, and then the other of them, but they did not speak or look at one another.

Jeffy crept in through the door like a shadow, and had arrived between them on the hearthrug before either of them was aware of him.

Then the rapturous welcome they gave him assured him of one thing. Even if it did not entirely calm his fears, he knew he had been much missed, and that they loved him very dearly.

6

A Rope Trick

Miss Amity and Little Lew could not do enough to show Jeffy how penitent they were, nor how thankful to have him home again.

This time Miss Amity made no rash promises, but fussed about him showing her affection, and being more than a trifle harsh with Little Lew.

The kitten insisted on sleeping on boards for another night 'To serve myself right!' as he put it, but he added, to Jeffy's distress: 'And if only I had my yellow handkersniff back you should have it for *your* bed, Jeffy, and I'd sleep on nothing at all!'

The kitten was now so respectful and humble Jeffy had not the heart to scold him, but much later that night he had a long and serious talk with Miss Amity about their joint responsibilities in bringing up Little Lew.

'He has no mother,' Jeffy pointed out. '*You* must be his mother! And he has no father, so I must take his place!'

'Oh what a lucky kitten he is!' cried Miss Amity, with heartfelt enthusiasm. 'We are going to be the best parents in the world!'

And so they were, for several weeks.

Little Lew grew, and got fat, and learnt to wash without being told to do so. He never stole food now, and was so obedient to Jeffy and Miss Amity that it looked as if they might one day become quite proud of him. So life went on in a very pleasant manner.

Jeffy no longer accompanied Miss Amity on her shopping expeditions. He had never really enjoyed them, whereas Little Lew liked to go, and enjoyed being patted on the head by the shopkeepers and the librarians and the ladies Miss Amity met along the way. He was becoming a remarkably handsome cat, though he was still very small for his age.

But one afternoon Jeffy found Miss Amity taking down the clothes-line and putting it into her shopping bag.

'What are you doing that for?' he asked in surprise. He had a feeling that Miss Amity had not wanted him to see her doing it.

'We need a new clothes-line,' snapped Miss Amity promptly. 'We must have had the old one for quite fifteen years!'

Before going out she picked up a ball of knitting wool from the kitchen dresser and put that in her shopping bag too.

'You can't be going to knit while you are out shopping,' said Jeffy in surprise.

'I need to match my knitting wool. I haven't enough to finish my stocking,' Miss Amity said.

'It's getting late, and it's raining,' said Jeffy. 'Why don't you leave it till the morning?'

'Oh no, I must have it tonight,' said Miss Amity hastily. 'Then I can do my washing early in the morning and hang it on the new line.'

'You can leave Little Lew with me, he'll only get wet,' said Jeffy, looking at the kitten asleep inside its box, but Miss Amity had already called it by name.

'What? What? I'm coming, Missammitty! I'm ready, I'm ready!' cried the kitten, leaping out of bed. Jeffy was puzzled to see it so eager and expectant about a walk to the shops in the rain.

'Shall I come with you?' he offered, uneasily.

'Oh no, Jeffy dear! You know you don't like shopping,' said Miss Amity very quickly, almost running out of the door in her mackintosh. 'We'll be back in half an hour. Not a minute longer!'

As she closed the door behind herself and the kitten Jeffy distinctly heard Little Lew say to her: 'That wouldn't do at all, Missammitty, would it?'

Extremely uneasy, Jeffy heard Miss Amity's footsteps fade away along the pavement. He could not settle down at all. Something was up between them! Something was wrong! And he tried to think of warning signs that he might have missed.

But Miss Amity had been taking extra pains to bring up Little Lew in the way he ought to go, and only that very morning she had announced: 'We came home by the prison as we always do on Fridays. Little Lew knows all about it now.'

Little Lew had snickered, and Jeffy had thought that a kitten might have its nose rubbed in warnings a little too often. It could become indifferent in the end.

But he had not said anything to Miss Amity.

And then, like a flash, the truth sprang into his head, and made everything daylight clear.

The prison! The rope! And the kitten's last words to Miss Amity! Without hesitation he rushed out of the door and down the street.

He took the road to the prison without a second thought. It was pouring with rain, and few people were about, but he kept constant watch ahead for the figure of Miss Amity carrying her shopping bag, with Little Lew trotting along at her heels. They were nowhere to be seen.

As he got nearer and nearer to the prison without catching up with them Jeffy's heart ceased to beat so wildly, and he felt more and more relieved. Perhaps after all they had gone shopping, and he had been wrong in his suspicions. He began to feel quite guilty at having misjudged Miss Amity.

He came face to face with the prison and its great gate, standing back across the square. The walls and the tower were lit up by floodlighting so that every brick stood out as clear as daylight. The few trees in the square around the building were growing well clear of the gates, and he could see nobody standing underneath them. There were no passers-by, and no sign at all of Miss Amity and Little Lew.

With a great sigh of thankfulness Jeffy turned to go home. He was already thinking about the warm fire he had left behind, and the saucer of milk he would receive on Miss Amity's return.

But just as he was turning away, something caught his eye. Nothing spectacular, nothing very unusual, in fact, just a dark blot on the prison wall, as if a spider were carefully making its way from brick to brick in the rain, dragging its spider's web behind it.

Jeffy blinked, and stared, and blinked again.

The spider, and it was a very large spider, was climbing steadily towards the top of the wall, and sometimes he could see the thread dangling behind it and sometimes he could not. In no time at all it was sitting on top of the wall, looking down, and pulling in its thread as fast as it would go.

Suddenly the thread gave place to something much thicker and stronger—it was no spider's web now, but a rope! And the spider was no spider at all, but Little Lew, perched on top of the prison wall and pulling up the rope with all his might, while the shadowy figure moving out from round the corner of the building and paying out the coils was one that Jeffy had known for nearly the whole of his life. It was Miss Amity! Jeffy rushed out into the square, but already it was too late.

The rope dropped over the wall; Little Lew slipped down it like a bead, and the next moment he and Miss Amity had vanished together round the corner.

Then a head appeared on top of the wall, followed by a pair of shoulders. A prisoner was escaping, and if he did not do something about it every convict inside the prison would be free before Jeffy could count his

nine lives.

He crossed the square like a flash of lightning, and made one tremendous leap for the alarm bell hanging in the archway of the prison door. As it clanged and clanged again he saw the first prisoner slide down the rope and run off, but before a second and a third could follow him, the warders were pouring out of the gates. The rope was pulled down. Jeffy saw the knitting wool break into a dozen pieces, as he dropped among the feet of the agitated warders, and quickly made his way home.

He hoped Miss Amity and Little Lew might be there before him, because however much he deplored and despised their behaviour he dreaded to have them captured and locked up, but they had not arrived. Probably they were lying low and waiting for the commotion to die down, when they might walk sedately home with their shopping.

Jeffy closed the door and waited for them in a state of great agitation. He could not settle down by the fire, and washing did not calm his feelings in the least.

When at last he heard footsteps and the door-handle turned he jumped up to receive them, not knowing exactly how he was going to express his indignation at their behaviour.

But it was not Miss Amity and Little Lew who opened the door. It was the escaped prisoner.

7

The Escaped Prisoner

Jeffy did his best to prevent the convict from coming in, but he just pushed past Jeffy, very nearly stepping on his tail.

'Mind out!' said Jeffy.

'Sorry, pusscat! Anyone at home?' said the prisoner, shutting the door behind him. 'Any money? Any food? Any clothes? I've got to get away from here quickly!'

'Missammitty is out,' said Jeffy firmly, 'and there is nothing for you here. You had better go away at once!'

'That depends if I can find what I need,' said the prisoner, looking all round the room. But at that very minute more footsteps came down the street.

Both Jeffy and the convict thought it was the police, but this time it *was* Miss Amity and Little Lew. The convict just had time to hide in the cupboard before they came in. And they were laughing.

'Oh Jeffy! Such an adventure! Such a wonderful, wonderful success!' Miss Amity said. 'You can't be angry when you hear what we have done! We rescued a prisoner out of the prison!'

'And he got away!' piped up Little Lew, quite beside himself with pride and excitement. 'Really he did! We saw him, Jeffy, we saw him!'

'That's all *you* know!' spluttered Jeffy. 'He's here now, in the cupboard!'

'No!' said Miss Amity, looking horrified. 'Then the police will come and I'll be arrested and so will Little Lew – oh Jeffy, what shall I do? What shall I do?'

'You should have thought of that before,' said Jeffy. 'I can't help you now.'

The convict opened the cupboard door and came out.

'Oh do go away! Do go away!' shrieked Miss Amity. 'I've done all I can for you – now leave me alone!'

'Well, I might go if you'll set me up with some food and some money,' the convict said unwillingly. 'I don't suppose you have any clothes that might fit me, being a lady?'

'Now look here,' said Jeffy, 'it's not going to help Missammitty even if you take all the food in the house and all the money. The police are bound to find her. They'll find the clothes-line and the knitting wool, and if they know you have been at the house and she has given you everything to get away with, well, I wouldn't wonder if they didn't shut her up for life. It doesn't seem fair, does it?'

'No,' the convict said reluctantly, 'it doesn't.'

'Not after getting you out like that,' said Jeffy.

'That's right!' agreed the convict.

'You wouldn't treat an old lady like that, would you?' said Jeffy. 'Not one that's old enough to be your grandmother?'

'Oh Jeffy,' wept Miss Amity, 'I'm *not* old enough

to be his grandmother!'

The convict was silent.

'Well, what do you want me to do about it?' he said at last.

'Give yourself up!' Jeffy urged. 'Go back to prison! Take your sentence like a man! You deserved it, didn't you? And you wouldn't let a lady take your punishment for you, would you? Not after rescuing you like that?'

There was a long silence before the convict spoke again.

'Well, no, I wouldn't,' he said at last.

'Oh thank you, thank you!' Miss Amity cried, taking both the convict's hands in her own. 'Oh what a gentleman you are! I shall never forget you, never! Such an example to Little Lew! Please do go back this minute with Jeffy to the prison before the police come and find you, and I'll be grateful to you for the whole of my life!'

With his head hung low between his shoulders, and Miss Amity's grateful kisses on his hands, the convict slouched out of the door in Jeffy's wake, with Miss Amity waving to him from the window. Little Lew, tired out, had gone to bed.

Jeffy saw the prisoner safely into the square in front of the prison, where he was received into the arms of half a dozen warders.

'Ah! Thought better of it, did you? No night to be on the run!' they said, escorting him back through the gates. 'Never mind, old man, nothing lasts for ever! One more day is over!'

Jeffy padded back to his home and went to bed without saying goodnight to Miss Amity.

In the morning he found himself being treated almost like an invalid. Miss Amity brought him a saucer of milk in the workbasket for breakfast. She and Little Lew talked to each other in whispers so that he would not be disturbed. Little Lew looked at him with large and pleading eyes, begging for forgiveness, and washed all over, ostentatiously, several times during the morning, from the top of his head to the tip of his tail, and then beginning at the beginning and doing it all over again, just to impress him, but Jeffy took no notice of him at all.

Miss Amity looked so miserable that he felt quite sorry for her, but he knew how easy it would be to forgive and comfort them both, so for their own good he ignored them, refused the milk, and turned his back on Little Lew's ablutions.

The atmosphere in the kitchen soon became very uncomfortable, between their penitence and the steam from Miss Amity's washing, which she was forced to dry on all the tables and chairs, because she had no clothes-line.

'I'll soon get you one, shall I?' Little Lew offered. 'There's lots in the gardens up the road!'

Miss Amity took him by the scruff of the neck, smacked him hard, and shut him in the coal hole.

'I would give a lot to know where that kitten was brought up,' she said to Jeffy.

Jeffy said nothing at all.

For several days he kept up a disapproving silence, until he realised that it no longer had any effect on Miss Amity, or on Little Lew. After a while they just forgot about him and talked to each other instead.

For the first few days they were very quiet and anxious to please, but presently their spirits rose, they laughed and teased each other, and made jokes that Jeffy did not like at all, about thieves and robbers stealing people's false teeth and other silly stories and goings-on. And when Little Lew was rolling on the floor with delight Miss Amity would become shame-faced, and scold herself, and say: 'But I mustn't talk like that in front of Jeffy. It's very wrong and wicked of me. Jeffy's a good cat, and his mother wouldn't like it! Naughty, naughty old me! How can you let me be so wicked, Lew?'

Jeffy just did not trust them at all.

And then one day they *robbed a bank*!

8

A Bank Robbery

This time Jeffy knew nothing at all about it until he saw the big letters on the boards outside the newspaper shop at the end of the road. That was because he had spent a long morning taking a walk by himself, down by the docks, as he so often did these days for exercise.

He always took great care to go in a different direction from Miss Amity and Little Lew, who he knew would be walking down the High Street meeting lots of people and having coffee with their friends.

A cat must have some exercise, besides which Jeffy's spirits these days were so low, and his daily life inside the house so depressing, that any change of air did him good. It was not that Miss Amity and Little Lew did not love him any more. They often went out of their way to show him that they did. But behind it all they were linked together by something that Jeffy could not describe, some force that bound one to the other and left Jeffy very much on the outside.

'Thick as thieves' was the expression that came reluctantly to his mind, though he did not like to use it.

'I shall go away and leave them,' he told himself a dozen times a week. But he never did.

Today he was coming back from his morning stroll when he read the placards outside the newspaper shop.

BANK ROBBED!
£1000 stolen from Bank in High Street!

He hoped Miss Amity and Little Lew would not read the posters. It might give them ideas.

When he arrived home dinner was on the table, but there was a suppressed air of excitement and agitation that went far beyond mere appetite. Little Lew was feverishly washing some extremely muddy paws, not that this was surprising, for he often went digging in the garden, but it was the way he was doing it that caught Jeffy's attention. It was as if he could not possibly clean them fast enough. And Miss Amity was rolling up what looked like some long, black stockings and bundling them into – of all places! – the bread bin!

'Why Jeffy, you're quite late!' Miss Amity cried as he came in. 'I was getting worried about you. I thought you might have got caught up in the terrible affair that has been happening in the town.'

'What terrible affair?' said Jeffy at once.

'The Bank Robbery!' said Miss Amity, smacking her lips, and brandishing the soup ladle rather like a flag. She was almost swelling with importance as she said it.

'The Bank Robbery!' echoed Little Lew, fixing large, excited eyes on Jeffy. 'A thousand pounds stolen!'

'A thousand pounds!' repeated Miss Amity in a hoarse whisper. *'A thousand pounds!* And the thieves got right away with it!'

'How terrible!' said Jeffy. 'And how wrong and disgraceful and wicked and reprehensible! Utterly reprehensible!'

'Reprehensiful!' repeated Little Lew. 'So terribly wicked and reprehensiful, wasn't it, Jeffy?'

'And don't you forget it!' said Jeffy, rounding on him. 'I hope they catch them soon! I expect they will!'

'Oh no, Jeffy, I'm sure they won't,' said Miss Amity. 'I'm sure the bank robbers were much too clever! Nobody recognised them, you see – they wore stockings over their faces, and they went into the Bank, and leaned over the counter . . . .'

'. . . And said: "Stick 'em up! Stick 'em up! This is a hold-up!"' squealed Little Lew, bouncing with excitement. 'And the cashiers thought they had guns, but it was only old carrots up their sleeves, so they handed over *a thousand pounds*! And the bank robbers ran away before the police came!'

The moment Miss Amity mentioned the stockings over their faces Jeffy knew who the bank robbers had been. He jumped on to the dresser and lifted the lid of the bread bin. There were two black stockings curled round the loaf of bread, and two old carrots lying underneath it.

'What have you done with the money?' Jeffy asked them fiercely.

But Miss Amity and Little Lew would not say. For a while they refused to admit to Jeffy that they had been the bank robbers. Miss Amity protested and cried, never quite saying No, she didn't or Yes, she did. Little Lew was just as bad.

'They thought it was a dog!' was the nearest he got to admitting anything about his part in the crime.

'You can see the money isn't here!' Miss Amity shouted in a rage, when she grew tired of being questioned by Jeffy. He began to think that they must have been part of a greater conspiracy. Somebody else must have been the master brain, and forced them into the crime, and had taken away the money afterwards. It helped him not to feel quite so badly about Miss Amity. After all, it was the excitement she was after, not the money.

But three days later when he was in the vegetable patch he saw that some of the Brussels sprout plants in the garden were wilting and dying; and this was not surprising, because their roots were sticking out of the soil, and under their roots something else was poking out of the earth, something that looked like the corner of a polythene bag.

Jeffy dug it up, and found it was indeed a polythene bag, full of banknotes. They were mostly ten pound notes, and all of them were new. They could only have come straight from the Bank. Jeffy counted them out, lying underneath the Brussels sprout plants where he could not be seen from the house.

While he thought what he was going to do, he washed.

After a long wash, he emptied the whole lot over the fence into the street and threw the bag over too. There was nobody in the street, but a strong wind was blowing, and he watched the notes whirling and dancing and tearing away in the direction of the Bank.

When he had replanted the Brussels sprouts and trodden them in firmly with all four paws, he went into the house.

'I found the money,' he told Miss Amity, 'and I threw it over the fence into the road. I expect the Bank will get it all back. I don't know if anybody saw where it came from, but if they did they are sure to tell the police. And this time I shall do absolutely nothing to save you. I don't want to be your cat any more.'

Miss Amity sobbed and wept and pleaded in vain. This time Jeffy would not forgive her. Little Lew kept well out of sight.

Miss Amity was also very frightened. She was quite positive that the banknotes would be traced back to her garden, and every time the postman or the milkman knocked, she thought it was the police coming to arrest her.

Jeffy lingered on for some days to see whether she would be arrested or not, but actually the wind had been so violent on that particular day, that nobody had the slightest idea where the money could have come from. Every single one of the notes was picked

up and returned to the Bank.

Jeffy ought to have left home at once, while his anger was still white hot against Miss Amity and Little Lew. Instead, he found his indignation slowly ebbing away, as the days passed by, and he saw them making such visible efforts to reform themselves and to make him happy.

Perhaps after all the great fright they had had while they waited for the police to come and apprehend them had done them some good. More and more often Miss Amity said that she was too old now to break the law.

'It's so sad not to be young any longer,' said Little Lew sympathetically, and wondered why Miss Amity shut him up in the coal cellar.

9

Kittens

Miss Amity told Jeffy that from now on she was going to change her way of living completely.

'I know I've been a wicked old woman,' she said. 'I can think of only two good things I've done in the whole of my life! One was taking you in, off the street, and the other was taking in Little Lew. I couldn't tell he was going to turn out a wrong-un, could I?'

'Well, no, I suppose you couldn't,' Jeffy agreed grudgingly. He remembered that he had encouraged her to take in Little Lew himself.

'I know there have been a terrible lot of bad things too,' Miss Amity said sadly, 'like Burglary and Thieving and Poaching and Pick-pocketing and Escaping Prisoners and Bank Robbering. But there are a whole lot of things I *haven't* done, Jeffy! You must give me credit for that! And from now on I'm going to concentrate on the two best ones. I'll never do any of the other things again. Never! You do believe me, don't you, Jeffy?'

Jeffy was silent. He did his very best to believe she meant what she said, and he was gentle but firm with Little Lew.

Each day saw the three of them becoming more friendly and companionable. They seemed to be growing into one happy, united family at last.

So Jeffy was not alarmed, but only a little surprised

when a few days later he saw Miss Amity coming down the street with a broad smile on her face, and an old perambulator simply filled to the brim with kittens. Little Lew was trotting at her heels.

'Sakes alive, Missammitty! What are you going to do with all those kittens?' Jeffy asked in amazement, for at times the house seemed hardly big enough to hold himself, Miss Amity and Little Lew.

'Just kittens,' said Miss Amity, tipping them out on to the kitchen floor. Jeffy distinctly heard a clink of glass as she did so, and Miss Amity hastily covered the bottom of the pram with newspapers.

'Beautiful kittens! *Special* kittens!' purred Little Lew with an impish look at Miss Amity, who trod sharply and not quite accidentally upon his paw.

'You needn't look so cross and suspicious!' she snapped at Jeffy. 'I'm not going to keep them here. Captain Macallister up the road is going to have them all at the Anchorage. He is very fond of little cats. I'm just going to give them some milk to drink to stop them yelling their heads off in the street.'

'I'd better go and tell him they are coming,' said Jeffy, but Miss Amity prevented him.

'I'll go myself,' she said. 'You give the kittens their tea.'

But when he had put each kitten's nose into a saucer of milk and set another for Little Lew Jeffy jumped up on to the pram and looked under the newspapers.

The perambulator was full of brandy bottles.

'What are you doing up there, Jeffy?' Miss Amity said, when she came back looking very pleased with herself.

'Brandy bottles! Smuggling! Contraband!' Jeffy spluttered. 'Where did you get them from, Missammitty? And how did you hide them from the Customs Officer?'

Miss Amity began to giggle.

'So easy!' she said. 'So very easy! The kittens, Jeffy, the kittens! Captain O'Sullivan put the bottles on the bottom and all his old cat's kittens on the top. They're a present for his old friend Captain Macallister. I'll take them along when the kittens have finished their tea. But I'm going back for another lot first.'

'Missammitty, I'm deeply ashamed of you! It's wrong, it's dreadfully wrong,' said Jeffy in great distress.

'What? Smuggling? Oh Jeffy, what's the harm in a little contraband when it means giving some kittens a good home?' said Miss Amity. 'The captain has promised to have all eight of the dear little things if I bring him two dozen bottles of brandy, and they are going to have a wonderful life at the Anchorage!'

After tea Miss Amity put the kittens back in the perambulator on top of the smuggled brandy bottles and the newspapers. Before going to Captain Macallister she went back to the docks, where she was to pick up the rest of the contraband, disguised in a bundle of washing.

The bundle was lying there waiting for her on the side of the wharf. Captain O'Sullivan and his boat were gone. Little Lew was skipping at Miss Amity's heels, but Jeffy followed at a great distance.

'Nice little kittens,' said a Customs Officer, strolling by and chucking Little Lew under the chin as Miss Amity picked up the washing. 'Well, ma'am, I hope the sun will shine for you tomorrow, when you air the Captain's pyjamas!'

Miss Amity went to the side of the dock to see whether the captain were still around and wanted her to take any more contraband. As soon as the Customs Officer disappeared she took a short walk along the dock in search of the boat. While she was searching Jeffy jumped on to the pram and gently dropped each one of the kittens on to the ground, lifting it out by the scruff of its neck.

Then he simply pushed the perambulator and all the contraband bottles into the dock. Little Lew leapt ten yards backwards in case he was pushed in too.

Miss Amity came running at the sound of the splash and so did the Customs Officer.

'We'll never get it back out of there,' he said, shaking his head gloomily as he looked into the water where the pram had vanished. 'It's too deep just there, and too awkward. One of our chaps dropped a case of whiskey in there by accident one day, on a trolley he was wheeling, and we never saw a sign of it again.'

Nothing came to the surface of the water except the newspaper, though Miss Amity waited for nearly an hour. And after that they all had to walk home, carrying the kittens.

This time it was Miss Amity who was angry with Jeffy, just as if she had forgotten all that they had meant to each other in the past and all that Jeffy had done for her.

'I don't know what I am going to say to Captain Macallister!' she stormed, as the kittens scuttled about the house, creating havoc. 'Eight kittens instead of his two dozen bottles of brandy! And to think of all the money I spent on buying that pram! I shall never forgive you, Jeffy, never!'

'That's all right! I am leaving you for good in any case!' said Jeffy.

And this time he did.

10

Train Robbers

Jeffy knew it was no good staying in the town or even in the district. It was so full of memories – happy memories, he felt bound to admit – of the days when he and Miss Amity had been friends and had lived quietly side by side, following a peaceful routine, that, if dull, had been so pleasant. He recalled the morning sorties down the High Street to the shops and the library, and frequent stops to chat with Miss Amity's friends, the half hours spent in the coffee shops. Sometimes it had felt tedious and a little boring, but how much better and happier than the later days, when Jeffy never knew what crisis was coming next?

He partly blamed himself for Little Lew's behaviour. Jeffy felt he ought to have been firmer from the beginning, when he might have turned Lew into a better influence, instead of a worse, on that side of Miss Amity that inclined towards crime, and revelled in the excitement of breaking the law. His mother, he felt sure, would have nipped all that in the bud.

But he had failed, and the two of them were in it, up to the hilt. He felt he could not protect them any longer by staying with them, and all he now wanted to do was to put as great a distance between Miss Amity, Little Lew and himself as it was possible to do.

Having hidden himself in warehouses and garages for the best part of a week, strongly resisting the temptation to go home and look through the window at night, Jeffy found his way to the railway station on a fine, frosty morning, and boarded a train for an unknown destination.

Until the train started and was actually under way he had to resist an almost uncontrollable impulse to jump out on to the platform and go home. But when the door of the guard's van was finally closed he knew he no longer had any choice, and it was almost a relief to have to follow his own destiny at last. The guard had made no objection at all to his travelling with the parcels and the mail.

'You can nab a few mice while you are about it,' he told him cheerfully, and Jeffy was only too glad to oblige, for he had been continually hungry since he left home.

The train gathered speed, the pistons thrust, the wheels rattled, the engine roared. Wisps of smoke flew past the cracks in the van door, and the agitated chuff-chuff-chuff sounded faster and faster. Jeffy felt as if he were travelling pressed against the flank of an enormous cat, much bigger than himself, that was carrying him away to some country of which he knew nothing at all. He could not imagine what would happen next, nor where the rest of his life would be spent. He had never pictured being in any other place but in Miss Amity's little house, in Miss Amity's street, in Miss Amity's town, as Miss Amity's favourite cat.

'Oh, Missammitty! Missammitty!' Jeffy cried, as a surge of homesickness for all that was past engulfed him like a wave. He burst into great sobs of misery, leaning against the mailbags, while the mice played round the parcels quite unafraid.

All of a sudden he was jerked into consciousness by a tremendous noise outside. The brakes were shrieking and clattering; the van shook and vibrated as if it were coming to pieces, as the train ground to a halt. Jeffy was thrown from one end of the van to the other with the mailbags on top of him, while at the same time the guard came running up the train along the corridors and burst into the van.

The next moment the doors were flung open, a gun was thrust inside, almost into the guard's face, and a fierce voice demanded:

'Come down from the train, please, guard, please, engine driver! Step outside while we get the mailbags! Don't resist! This is a hold-up and we have got you covered! Hands above your heads IF YOU PLEASE!'

The two figures standing on the side of the track outside the van, one tall, one short, were unmistakably train robbers. Both wore masks and dark clothes, and the gun had every appearance of being a real one.

They were holding up the engine driver and the guard as if they intended to shoot if they were not instantly obeyed, and while the guard stepped slowly down on to the track with his hands above his head

Jeffy struggled out from beneath the mailbags and crouched in the shadows, washing furiously as he tried to think what to do. The robbers were marching the driver and the guard about a hundred yards away from the train, intending to tie them up before stealing the mailbags out of the van.

Suddenly Jeffy gathered his wits together. He dropped lightly on to the track, galloped beside the train to the footplate, and leapt aboard the engine. As he raised himself on to his hind paws he could see nothing in front of him but a vast panel of knobs, each one larger and shinier than the other, but he did not hesitate for a moment. Down the train came cries and shouts and banging of doors as the passengers began to realise that something critical was happening. They poked their heads out of the windows to see for themselves what had so suddenly stopped the train.

Jeffy pulled knob after knob in desperation. Steam spurted, hooters screamed, lights went off and on. Suddenly the train shuddered all over. There came an enormous jerk, then a jolt, and then another. The wheels began to turn, and great balloons of smoke shot into the sky. Faster and faster turned the wheels, and the coaches rattled as the train gathered speed.

The rattle of the train was accompanied by the loud cheering of the passengers, who were just beginning to realise what danger had been threatening them, and how nearly they had escaped a train robbery by two remorseless thieves. Turning his head for one

moment, Jeffy saw the two black figures come tearing towards the track, as if at the last moment they meant to hurl themselves through the doors of the guard's van, but the train was moving too fast for them.

Yet in that brief moment before the train disappeared round the bend in a cloud of smoke, Jeffy recognised with horror the unmistakable figures of Miss Amity and Little Lew, their gloved fists waving furiously at the vanishing train.

He stayed on the footplate just long enough to run the train into the next large station. Then he pulled all the knobs until the engine ceased to draw the coaches. As it drew up beside the platform he slipped quietly out of the engine driver's cab on to the tracks on the far side of the train.

11

Jeffy's New Home

In the days that followed Jeffy haunted the station, making himself as inconspicuous as possible, but keeping his ears wide open for news of his one-time friends. Nobody took much notice of a stray cat in the waiting-room or restaurant, or sitting in the doorway of the station master's office with one ear cocked to the news bulletin on the radio, while it seemed to be watching the sparrows.

The news that he expected came at last, though it nearly broke his heart to hear it blared out across the platform on the one o'clock programme. The train robbers had been caught. Miss Amity had tried her luck too far, and this time Jeffy could not save her from paying the price of her wickedness.

He had no idea where they had taken her and Little Lew, but when at last the trial was over Jeffy heard the result on the station master's radio set. Miss Amity and Little Lew were sent to prison for ten years each. It would have been longer, the Judge said, if Little Lew had been older, or if Miss Amity had been younger. He hoped that the rest of their lives would be spent in mending their ways.

Since he now had no home Jeffy continued to live at the station, but every train that thundered by reminded him of that dreadful day, and he would start out of sleep thinking he saw again those once loved figures holding up the train, and waving their fists as they were whisked out of sight.

Presently it became too much for him to bear, and he quietly disappeared. The station master, who had grown fond of him, called him in vain, putting out scraps night and morning that were never eaten. He thought that Jeffy must have been run over somewhere up the track. He was very sorry but there was nothing he could do about it now.

Jeffy plodded across country, up hill and down dale, not caring where he went nor whether he lived or died. Only his early training made him keep himself clean and tidy, so that anyone who saw him took him for a domestic cat that was taking a day off hunting.

If he had known which prison Miss Amity was in he would have gone to live close by. The Governor might even have allowed him to become a prison cat and share their punishment. But he did not know, and Miss Amity was certainly not in the men's prison beside their old home. After searching in various towns Jeffy gave it up and kept to country places where he was not molested by other toms or threatened by buses and motorcycles. And it was difficult to find anything to eat in the towns. Every dustbin seemed to have a claimant cat, while in the country there was always the odd mouse to be found. Not that he cared whether he ate or not, but there was always the haunting feeling that Miss Amity might need him when she came out of prison, and he must keep himself alive for that happy day.

Winter came and it was very cold.

The earth froze. In the woods mice and birds found shelter in thick bushes and Jeffy had nothing to eat. He had to leave the country and go back into the town, just in the hope of finding enough food to keep himself from starving.

He came in sight of a city built round a large and towering building looking so tall and formidable in the winter twilight that his heart began to throb with excitement. Those high walls, those narrow windows, those doors studded with big, fat nails, surely that could only be a prison? And would it be, could it be the prison that contained Miss Amity and Little Lew?

Jeffy hurried across the frosty fields into the outskirts of the town and threaded his way through the busy streets towards the great building he had seen.

But as he got near he began to have doubts. The windows were not so narrow as he had expected, and instead of iron bars the light inside them shone out through coloured glass and made patterns on the grass outside. There came the sound of happy singing from within, and Jeffy recognised that it was not a prison at all but a great cathedral. Just as he reached the entrance the door opened and out poured the evening's congregation, while behind them the cathedral organ pealed a voluntary, and one by one the lights were dimmed and then put out in the aisles and nave.

Jeffy waited aimlessly until the organist came out, talking to the Bishop, and because the Bishop looked kindly and had a gentle voice, he followed him home across the green to his house. He suddenly felt so lonely, so homeless and abandoned, that even to listen to a human voice became a comfort to him.

The Bishop was a kind, compassionate old man, and he too was lonely. Finding Jeffy at his heels he invited him to come and share his home, asking no questions, but treating him with the utmost kindness and consideration.

Jeffy's gratitude knew no bounds. Slowly his fur grew thick and shining again, his ribs no longer showed through his skin, and his eyes gleamed once more. But he always looked a little sad and wistful.

The Bishop knew that Jeffy had something on his mind, but he left him alone, knowing that he would probably talk about it in his own good time.

If only he could have forgotten about the past, Jeffy would have been quite content to spend the next ten years of his life in the Bishop's parlour, sometimes hearing about cathedral affairs, and sometimes about the Bishop's boyhood and schooldays, which he loved to relate to his cat. Jeffy became well-known and respected in the cathedral close, trotting at the Bishop's heels, much as, long ago, he used to trot behind Miss Amity.

And so, almost unnoticed, the time went by.

The Bishop was in the habit of reading aloud little

bits of news to Jeffy from the evening papers as they sat together by the fire.

One evening he exclaimed in surprise: 'Well, I never did! How time runs by! The train robbers who attempted to steal the mailbags on the Shantylands express have been freed!'

Jeffy sat bolt upright, his whiskers standing on end.

The Bishop did not notice his agitation and went on reading: '. . . Having served half of their sentences the two prisoners have been released on grounds of good conduct and genuine regret for the deed they intended to commit. Their release having taken place, they have left the prison with the Governor's blessing on their future welfare.'

Jeffy was washing himself in the greatest excitement and agitation. The Bishop went on to read the cricket scores, but Jeffy did not listen.

Five years! Five years had gone by, and at last his dear Missammitty was free again! Five years he himself had spent in comfort in the Bishop's home, being fed and cherished and cared for. No cat could wish for a better home in which to end his days.

But at the thought of Miss Amity going back to the little home they had shared together the years fell away like leaves behind him as Jeffy longed with all his heart and soul to rush to her side and join her there.

But how could he leave the Bishop? The old man was no longer young, and he depended more and more on Jeffy. He was always telling him so.

'I don't know how I used to get on without you, Jeffy!' he would say. 'Not having the blessing of a wife, there was no one to talk to. I was a very solitary old man before you arrived. But since you came into my life I have never been lonely at all.'

'I was lonely too, Bishop, till you took me into your home,' Jeffy told him, 'and I will never leave you by yourself again!'

But now that was what he wanted most of all in the world to do!

All that evening poor Jeffy was so restless and unhappy that at last the Bishop could hardly fail to notice his distraction.

'Now, Jeffy,' he admonished him very kindly, 'that is the fifteenth time you have washed all over! I think you must have something on your mind!'

'Sometimes . . . ' said Jeffy, looking in the opposite direction, 'sometimes I can't help thinking about days gone by . . . .'

'Ah!' said the Bishop. 'Don't we all? And we have such regrets, don't we, Jeffy? Such bitter regrets! But no, you could never have regrets, my dear Jeffy . . . a wise, upright little cat like yourself.'

'Oh I have, I have!' burst out Jeffy. 'You see, once I had a friend – a dear, dear friend –' He broke off, and the Bishop waited patiently. Jeffy washed his ears very violently and then settled down by the fireside, looking up into the Bishop's face.

'She was the best friend I ever had in my life,' said Jeffy, 'next to you!'

'And did you lose your friend?' asked the Bishop gently.

'Well, not exactly,' said Jeffy. 'It was a case of desertion. You see, I left my friend. I let my friend go – for ever!'

'How sad!' said the Bishop in sympathy. 'And now you regret it so bitterly! I can well understand it. It is sad to let one's friends slip out of one's life, very sad indeed.'

'Even if . . .' whispered Jeffy. 'Even if one happened to be friends with . . . a burglar?'

'Oh yes,' said the Bishop. 'It would still be sad.'

'Or . . . a thief?'

'Still sad. Very sad.'

'Or a poacher? Or a prison buster? Or a pick-pocket? Or a smuggler? Or a bank robber? Or a *train robber?*' said Jeffy in a rush.

'I think that always, always one should hold fast to one's friends,' said the Bishop. 'Of course one need not approve of their behaviour, and one should say so, and always try to help them to do better. But desert them – never.'

'But I did! I did!' burst out Jeffy, and he told the Bishop the whole story.

'I can't really blame you, Jeffy,' said the Bishop when he had finished. 'I don't see how you could have acted otherwise at that time. You did all you could to help your dear friend Miss Amity, and Little Lew. And one should not judge other people when one is imperfect oneself. It would surprise you, Jeffy, to know how many times in my life I have been tempted. For years, I have longed, I have *yearned* – to become a highwayman!'

Jeffy stared at the Bishop as if he could not believe his ears.

The Bishop nodded, staring straight into the fire.

'I imagined creeping out into the night, my work in the cathedral over for the day, nobody recognising me in my disguise of long ago,' the Bishop mused, half aloud, 'with a mask over my eyes and a pistol in my pocket – not a real one, of course! Making my way by stealth to the Great North Road, and while all the town thought their Bishop was asleep in bed I would be out there holding up the cars and coaches: "Your money or your life! Hands up! Hands up! Hand over your valuables and no harm shall come to you!"'

The Bishop became so excited that he seized the poker and began to brandish it at Jeffy. 'Of course I would have given them all back afterwards,' he added, dropping the poker.

'And did you really do it?' asked Jeffy, awestruck.

'Oh no, never,' said the Bishop. 'But it was just my secret dream. So you see I can understand what made your Miss Amity seek for adventure, even though it was so very wrong. I can't prevent half of me from crying, "Hurrah! Hurrah!" when you tell me about it, even though the rest of me is saying: "How could she?" – I'm afraid I can't be a very good Bishop!'

Jeffy looked at him with sympathy, until with an effort the Bishop spoke again.

'Jeffy! I know which way your duty lies, and so do you. It is time for you to go back to your friend. Your Miss Amity will need you now, more than ever she has done before. Life will not be easy for her when she comes out of prison. Her friends and acquaintances may not want to know her. Homes where she once was welcome may close their doors on her, and people may turn their backs in the street. She will need your help and support, because you were once her friend, and her friend you must be again. This time for ever.'

'But what about you, Bishop?' said Jeffy, remembering all the kindness he had received in the past five years. 'You are my friend too. I can't keep on deserting everybody.'

'Never mind about me,' said the Bishop bravely. 'I shall go on as I did before I met you. But if ever the time comes that your Miss Amity wants a friend in need, I shall be very pleased and honoured to offer her all the help in my power.'

It was dark and it was raining. Out of sheer gratitude to the Bishop, Jeffy put off going to find Miss Amity until daylight the next morning. He fell asleep to happy dreams of life beginning all over again, only better than ever, as in the best of the days gone by.

12

Where is Miss Amity?

In the morning Jeffy left the Bishop's house, promising that whatever the future held he would come back and visit his friend as soon as possible.

It was a long, long way to his old home. Jeffy had not realised how far he had travelled since the hold-up. It took him over a week to cover the distance on foot.

Slowly the landscape took on a more familiar appearance. The line of the hills made a pattern he used to look at, far-off, from Miss Amity's windows, and presently the faint, fishy smell of the docks came to meet him on the breeze. He could not be very far from home.

He turned the corner of the well-known street almost before he realised it, and there, half-way down the pavement, was the familiar gate, more shabby than ever, as if no one had put any paint on it for a long, long time.

Jeffy broke into a gallop, and was underneath the gate in twenty long leaps from the top of the street.

But the door of Miss Amity's house was fast closed, and so was the kitchen window through which he had often peered. A large board was propped against the sill, and on the board was printed in large red letters:

SOLD.

It was such a shock to Jeffy that he sat back on his haunches staring at the board, as if he could hardly believe his eyes. The letters seemed to jump up and down in front of his vision as if he could not focus on them. When at last he dragged his gaze away he found he was being stared at in his turn by a large ginger and white tomcat that he vaguely remembered having met as a small and cheeky kitten when he lived there with Miss Amity, five years ago.

'Looking for your folks?' the ginger cat enquired.

'I am looking for Miss Amity,' Jeffy said, breathless. 'She used to live here once.'

'She's been gone a long time now,' said the ginger cat, pretending to wash. Jeffy could see that it hardly knew how.

'I know!' he said. 'She's been gone five years! I lived with her myself, and it was just five years ago.'

'She's been back once,' said the ginger cat, after a pause.

'When? When? When?'

The ginger cat considered.

'Must be a week ago,' it said, yawning.

Jeffy nearly jumped out of his skin.

'Did you speak to her? Did you see her leave? Did you ask her where she was going?' he demanded.

'Yus!' said the ginger cat laconically.

'Then what? What? What? What did she tell you?' Jeffy cried.

'She didn't say nothing!' returned the cat sulkily.

'Stuffy old lady! And that goes for her smut of a cat too! But I kept an eye on her,' he added with cunning, pausing in his makeshift washing, 'and I saw her write something on the window, underneath the board.'

Jeffy was up on the window-sill in a flash. He pushed his head under the sales board and heard it fall to the ground with a crash.

Written in the dust of the window pane, which seemed not to have been cleaned for years, was the one word EMIGRATED.

'Whatever that may mean,' said the ginger cat.

But Jeffy had not lived with the Bishop for nothing. Every night he had listened to crossword clues, and even helped to look up words in the dictionary. He knew that EMIGRATED meant GONE TO LIVE ABROAD PERHAPS FOR EVER.

Jeffy began to cry.

Embarrassed, the ginger tomcat went away. Jeffy was left alone on Miss Amity's window-sill.

13

On Board

After a while Jeffy stopped crying and began to wash. In spite of the ominous words written on the window pane he felt closer to Miss Amity than he had done for many a year past.

Only a week ago she had been standing where he was standing now. It was her own finger that had written on the window pane, and her own footmarks were still faintly imprinted on the soil underneath the sill, while beside them were the small, round paw-marks of Little Lew.

Surely nobody could emigrate very far in just seven days? If he could only find them now they might still live happily for ever after. But going to live abroad meant leaving the country, and leaving the country meant getting on a boat, or in an aeroplane, or swimming for a very long way across the sea. Jeffy did not think that Miss Amity would be able to afford to travel in an aeroplane, and swimming was out of the question, both for herself and Little Lew.

It seemed much more likely, therefore, that she would have gone to the docks to find a boat that would take her abroad, and somebody there might have seen her, and would be able to tell him something about her.

Jeffy left his old home and followed the road to the docks.

For two days he roamed up and down the quayside, looking for signs of his friends, and listening to the conversation of the sailors. Nobody could tell him anything about them. All he learned was that the other side of the world was a very long way away.

Miss Amity and Little Lew were already several days ahead of him. He dared not wait any longer. When he saw that a passenger ship was getting ready to leave on a cruise to tropical islands he ran lightly up the gang-plank and offered himself as ship's cat to the Captain.

'Good cat or bad cat?' the Captain asked at once.

'Good cat,' said Jeffy humbly.

'Ah!' said the Captain. 'They all say that! Then they catch one mouse and the moment we put out to sea they do nothing more than lie in the sun or plague the cook for titbits! How do I know you are any better than any other cat?'

Jeffy bowed his head. He did not know how to prove to the Captain that he meant to work his best and do just what was expected of him.

'What was the first thing your mother ever taught you?' barked the Captain, impressed that Jeffy had not answered him back or been cheeky to him.

'Always be clean and tidy!' Jeffy answered at once. 'Always be honest . . . never take what doesn't belong to you, not-once-not-ever . . . think before you act and wash before you think!'

'Well, well!' said the Captain, quite impressed.

'That's a mouthful of good intentions. But where are your references?'

'My what?' said Jeffy, startled.

'Your character! Hasn't somebody given you a reference about your being of good character?' the Captain demanded. 'Didn't you bring one with you?'

It had not occurred to Jeffy that such a thing might be necessary.

'I'm afraid not,' he said regretfully.

'I don't think I could take you on board without a reference,' said the Captain finally. 'How do I know you are really sober, diligent, honest, hardworking, competent and trustworthy? I only have your word for it!'

'I am sure my late master the Bishop would have given me that kind of character, if he had known it was necessary,' said Jeffy, preparing to leave.

'So your master was a Bishop, was he?' said the Captain, taking notice. 'Why did you run away to sea and leave him then?'

'I didn't run away,' Jeffy explained. 'I had the Bishop's blessing to go and look for some old friends of mine. But I find they have emigrated.'

'Ah!' said the Captain, relieved. 'So you think your Bishop would have guaranteed you to be of good character, do you?'

'I am sure he would,' said Jeffy modestly.

'Very well, you can stay on board,' said the Captain. 'Don't plague the passengers. Go to the cook once a day for food, and keep the whole place free from mice. I'll give you your passage for nothing.'

Jeffy's eyes shone with gratitude. He left the Captain's cabin and set about making himself as useful and as inconspicuous as possible. Soon afterwards the ship left the dock for the open sea.

True to the Captain's instructions Jeffy avoided the passengers and spent most of his time, when not mousing, sitting on a bollard in a shadowy corner of the deck watching the everlasting sea. What he looked for Jeffy could not have explained. He did not really expect to see Miss Amity and Little Lew sailing or rowing themselves across the wide ocean, and yet a fear that he might miss them if they *were* there drove him back always to his look-out post, and even during the hours of darkness one saw him still sitting there, gazing at the horizon. Even when he washed, his eyes never left the sea, and he ate all his meals looking oceanwards, taking little notice of the gulls that wheeled and cried above his head.

If his heart had not been so full of anxiety Jeffy would have enjoyed the voyage as much as any travels he had yet experienced. His work was not too hard. After the first day or two the mice seemed to have been completely banished from the ship. The crew were very kind and friendly. They nicknamed him the Bishop, which embarrassed Jeffy a little, until he realised they were doing it out of respect for his late master.

The cook offered him the very choicest scraps from the kitchen pans, and fed him, not once, but two or three times a day. The Captain stopped to stroke or speak to him whenever he passed Jeffy's look-out post, and never failed to call him: 'Good cat! Good cat!' which made Jeffy's heart swell with pride and appreciation. He made frantic efforts to catch and kill more and more mice, hunting for them in the darkest and deepest corners of the ship, and, when he had disposed of them, laying out their tails on the deck for the Captain to judge for himself how determined Jeffy was to please and to be useful.

Not that the Captain had any doubts, by now, of Jeffy's value.

'A fine cat! A good, excellent cat!' he told the mate. 'Worth its weight in gold! But then, you would expect that of a Bishop's cat, wouldn't you?'

One afternoon the sea around the ship as far as the horizon lay spread out so wide and calm and blue that Jeffy could see for a dozen miles in all directions. As there was nothing solid to be seen on all the vast surface around him Jeffy left his favourite watch tower for a few minutes to go hunting in the hold that held the baggage, in case a few mice, or even a rat, might still be hiding there. He had not found any for some days, and he was a little nervous that the Captain might get rid of him at the first port of call if he thought he was not earning his keep. Of course the Captain would have done nothing of the kind, but

Jeffy's conscience would not let him accept so much kindness while offering nothing in return.

He ran down the ladder to the hold and prowled round the stacks of trunks and suitcases, sniffing carefully, and listening for the first, faint rustle of a mouse.

Suddenly his whiskers twitched, his ears shot forwards, and he stopped short with one paw in the air, half doubled-up under his chest.

Behind a very large cabin trunk something had stirred.

Jeffy waited, but when nothing more happened he eased himself forward as smoothly and silently as a trickle of oil, hugging the side of the trunk and sliding past the end of it.

The trunk stood a little apart from the rest of the baggage, and he fully expected to see an escaping mouse dart when he put his head and whiskers round the corner of it. His limbs were all tensed to spring and pounce, for he knew that no mouse could escape him once he had sighted it. But there was no mouse to be seen.

Jeffy circled the whole trunk, his flanks pressed close to its sides, his velvet feet soft and noiseless, one placed silently behind the other, his whiskers sensing his way in the dim light of the hold.

Again came the rustling sound. It did not come from round the corner but was close to his ear, *inside* the trunk, and when he raised himself upon his hind legs Jeffy could see that the lid was not quite closed – it was propped open just wide enough to allow a mouse, or several mice, to run in and out of the crack.

They must be creating havoc inside, Jeffy thought. Probably they had already made their nests there.

This would never do. Mouse nests inside the passengers' luggage could not be tolerated. The Captain would be held responsible, and he in turn would blame Jeffy.

And I *am* responsible, thought Jeffy, and I must get inside that trunk as quickly as possible and get rid of the mice.

The gap between the lid and the trunk was very small, but where a mouse could slither Jeffy could also slide a paw. He followed the first paw with the second, and then thrust his whole head into the gap and peered inside.

The next moment his heart nearly leapt out of his body as the trunk lid sprang up and fell backwards with a bang! Something black leapt upwards to meet him . . . something smaller and even blacker bounced into his face, and two well-known voices, hysterical with joy and excitement called his name:

'Jeffy! Oh Jeffy! Jeffy!'

Dazed with joy, and almost paralysed by disbelief, Jeffy realised that Miss Amity and Little Lew were actually climbing out of the trunk and fighting for the privilege of being the first to hug him round the neck.

14

The Stowaways

When Jeffy realised that his search was at an end, and he had actually caught up with his dear friends before the voyage was halfway over, he glowed with happiness and relief. He purred and purred in Miss Amity's arms, meanwhile licking Little Lew with a warm and loving tongue, and wondering however the little fellow had managed to get himself so dirty. Lew soon told him.

'We've been here for days and days and days,' he babbled. 'Oh, Jeffy, it has been so dreadful! We've eaten all our food we brought out of the house with us. We finished it long ago. We're getting so hungry, Jeffy! Oh, Jeffy, you can't imagine how hungry we are!'

With a pang of dismay Jeffy realised that the loved friends he had been looking for so anxiously were in fact stowaways on board the ship, and what the Captain would have to say about it he could not imagine. But for the moment he could only think of the joy of being re-united with them again.

'Why did you do it . . . oh why?' he asked them fondly.

'We wanted to start life all over again in another country. We would leave all our wickedness behind us,' Miss Amity said, stroking her long-lost Jeffy as if she could never let him go. 'I thought you wouldn't want to see me ever again, Jeffy dear, after I came out of prison. I thought you would rather forget about me. I had disgraced you and let you down. I thought you couldn't possibly care for me any more. And if I went to another country you would be able to forget all the trouble I brought on you, and I would make a fresh beginning, far, far away. Besides, I had to think of Little Lew. It was better for him to make a new life in a new country than to be reminded all the time of the way we used to live before. I missed you so badly, Jeffy dear, all those long, sad years, but I thought it was for the best. I sold the house before I came on board, so I can't go back there anyway. There is nowhere else for us to go.'

'And we are so *hungry*!' wailed Little Lew at the top of his voice.

'Hush! The sailors will hear you,' warned Jeffy. 'I'll bring you some food.'

He watched Miss Amity and Little Lew scramble back inside the trunk before he pattered up the ladder from the hold and went straight to the kitchen.

It was unlike Jeffy to hang about the cook's heels asking for his dinner, but he did not ask in vain. The cook offered him half a fowl, which in the ordinary way Jeffy would have thought excessive, but now he almost snatched it in his delight, and hurried back to deliver it to his friends waiting impatiently for him in the hold.

'Is that all?' whined Little Lew, smacking his lips

when his share was done. 'You must live a wonderful life, Jeffy, with all those passengers dropping you bits and pieces! I bet you eat like a prince, don't you, Jeffy?'

'Lewsy! Don't be so rude!' said Miss Amity severely. 'After prison food everything tastes so delicious,' she apologised to Jeffy. 'But I haven't had time to polish his manners since we came out. Thank you, thank you, Jeffy dear! How good to us you are, and we are so undeserving! Don't bother about us any more, my dear, till we arrive in port. Surely we shall soon get to some foreign country or another, and then we can all join up again and be happy, as we were in the good old days. Oh Jeffy, you don't know what it means to me to see you again!'

'I will bring you food three times a day,' Jeffy promised. 'That is, whenever the cook feeds me. I don't mix with the passengers myself, and they never give me bits and pieces. The cook gives me food in the morning and in the middle of the day and in the evening. I will bring it to you, and at least it will keep you from starving. You will both have to stay very quiet while I am away, because I don't think the Captain would be very pleased to know that you are here.' And indeed his feelings were very mixed as he left them and climbed back to the deck.

Jeffy was overjoyed at finding his dear Miss Amity again, and even Little Lew, but he would much rather not have found them as stowaways. All night long he tossed and turned, wondering whether to take the Captain into his confidence and beg mercy for them, but the fact remained that Miss Amity and Little Lew were not only stowaways, but they were also ex-criminals, with a considerable list of crimes to their names, and Jeffy was pretty certain that they would be anything but welcome on board the pleasure cruiser.

When morning came he still had not resolved the problem, but he was early at the kitchen door, and carried a whole kipper down to the hold.

Miss Amity picked at her share gratefully. Little Lew gobbled and choked and spat bones and asked for more. Jeffy did not think his manners bad been improved by his stay in prison.

Lew was also bored. He got out of the trunk and pranced about among the pieces of luggage making quite a noise, which Jeffy thought was very unwise.

'The sailors may hear you,' he warned him.

'But I'd tell them I was your little foster-brother,' said Lew, his eyes shining with devotion.

'That wouldn't make any difference,' said Jeffy, gloomily shaking his head.

'What would they do to me?' Little Lew asked curiously.

'Put you in a basket and sling you overboard, most likely!' Jeffy replied. This silenced Little Lew for the meantime. He crept back inside the cabin trunk and went to sleep.

Because he brought all the food the cook gave him to his friends, Jeffy, of course, went without. At first he felt well able to live on the fat he had accumulated during the voyage, but presently he grew very hungry. Miss Amity and Little Lew ate everything that he brought to them, and Lew always pleaded for more. Jeffy found himself haunting the ship's kitchens in between mealtimes, in the hope of finding some scraps for himself. He even found his way into the dining-saloon to pick up bits from the floor. This was just what the Captain had told him not to do, and he felt very ashamed, especially when some of the sailors' remarks came to his ears:

'The old cat's getting quite greedy,' they said to one another.

At last he brought the joyful news to the hold that the ship was expected to berth at some tropical island within the next three days.

'Three days!' exclaimed Miss Amity. 'I thought we were bound to reach dry land before that. I don't know how I'm going to go on doing nothing for a whole three days longer. You don't know what it's like, Jeffy, being shut up down here. It's worse than prison!'

'Much worse!' echoed Little Lew. 'And I'm so hungry!'

Jeffy left them below, feeling heartless, but there was nothing more that he could do for them. The cook had not been quite so friendly to him of late. Having tripped over Jeffy a couple of times he seemed tired of seeing him hanging round the kitchen, and threw his food out onto the deck. Sometimes the bits and pieces were not very fresh. Miss Amity never complained, but Little Lew did, constantly. It was all that Jeffy could do to prevent him from leaving the hold and going up to forage for himself.

One day, when Jeffy and Miss Amity were quietly talking about days gone by, they realised that Little Lew had disappeared and was nowhere to be found in the whole length and breadth of the hold. Jeffy searched for him calling his name, and growing more and more anxious, when all of a sudden the little cat came flying down the ladder from the deck above, making such a racket that for a moment Miss Amity thought the entire heap of baggage was falling about her ears.

Little Lew was half trembling and half giggling. His fur was standing on end and he kept glancing backwards over his shoulder as he ran. Once arrived, he leapt inside the cabin trunk and tried to cover himself with the contents.

Heavy footsteps could be heard pursuing him, and Jeffy hastily thrust Miss Amity into the trunk after Lew, and closed the lid on the pair of them.

Only just in time too, for the next moment one of the sailors came thundering down the ladder. He stopped short when he saw Jeffy in the hold.

'Don't tell me it was you I saw all the time!' he

exclaimed. 'I must have been dreaming! I could have sworn it was a black kind of cat – scraggy like and not so handsome. Much, much smaller than you. Have you got a pal down here, Bishop? Let's have a look!'

The sailor stamped around the hold, but the trunk lid was fast closed and the occupants remained quite motionless. Not until the sailor had disappeared did Jeffy open the lid a chink, propping it with a rag, before the two hidden inside could suffocate.

'There! You see what you have done!' he scolded Little Lew. 'You have put your life in danger, and Miss Amity's! The Captain will certainly throw you overboard if he finds you are here. Why couldn't you stay down here as I told you?'

'Oh I am so sorry, Jeffy, so sorry,' moaned Little Lew. 'I did just long to see a little bit of sunshine again – I felt I was going blind in all this darkness. And there were such lovely smells coming from the kitchen galley. I just thought there might be a tiny little something for me to eat! How could I tell that the cook would fall over me, and that a sailor would catch sight of me as I ran away?'

'Well, let's hope no harm is done,' said Jeffy. 'But they are bound to be suspicious now, and you must never, never, *never* do it again!'

'No, Jeffy! I won't, Jeffy!' promised Little Lew.

But he broke his promise the very next morning.

15

Hijackers

Balmy breezes, blue skies, and the waft of strange and spicy scents on the air announced their arrival among tropical islands.

Jeffy lay on deck in the shade, trying to pretend to himself that he was not hungry. He had carried all his breakfast down to the hold, but there had not been enough of it to keep a mouthful for himself.

By midday his hunger pains became excessive, and he found himself creeping towards the kitchen, feeling very guilty, but hoping that there might be some morsel going begging, and a kind pair of hands ready and willing to throw it to him.

As he peeped round the galley door, he found the kitchen nearly empty, except for the horrifying picture of Little Lew, just arrived there, and on the point of leaping on the table to plunge his head inside one of the cooking-pots.

Jeffy let out a miaow of protest, while at the same time the cook came bustling in from the store-room carrying a bag of flour and the rolling pin. He saw Jeffy and Little Lew at one and the same moment, and hurled first the rolling pin and then the bag of flour at them both.

Lew was nearest to him. The rolling pin missed him, but the bag of flour caught him fair and square. It burst open on his sides, just as he rushed to take

FLOUR

shelter behind Jeffy. The two of them fled for their lives. Little Lew made for the ladder leading to the hold, but Jeffy ran a few yards only, and then, in order to cover Little Lew's flight, he turned to face the cook, and took the whole force of his fury on his own head.

The cook was not an unjust man, and he had not seen Jeffy himself eating out of his precious saucepans, but there had been a cat there, a strange cat, and therefore the cat must have had something to do with Jeffy. He stood cursing Jeffy with all his might and main, till Jeffy's ears drooped in disgrace, and he flattened himself on the deck, wondering what on earth was going to happen to them all now.

Summoned by the cook's curses the other sailors gathered round to listen, and Jeffy trembled all over as he heard them decide to make a thorough search of the hold the minute that the morning's duties were done.

'Shall I report it to the Captain, Cookie?' said the mate, but the cook advised waiting until they had caught and captured the strange cat among themselves. Jeffy crept away in deep humiliation to brood and worry and to count the minutes until his friends would be discovered and brought to justice.

The morning passed all too quickly. Hardly had the last passenger left the dining-saloon than a large group of sailors, armed with mops and brooms, emerged threateningly from the kitchen quarters, and advanced along the deck towards the hold.

Jeffy was ahead of them like a streak of lightning, to warn Miss Amity and Little Lew that they must close the lid of the trunk and lie as still as mice until the search was over.

But before he had reached the first rung of the ladder, with the party of sailors hard upon his heels, some dark and dual force surged up from the darkness below, nearly knocking him head over heels as they burst upon the deck.

Dressed in a weird assortment of hats and garments, with their faces masked and their hands flourishing swords, pistols, and other weapons discovered among the baggage below, Miss Amity and Little Lew strode into the sunlight and faced the group bearing down on them to arrest them.

Already Jeffy recognised Miss Amity in her most formidable and dangerous mood.

'This is a hijacking!' Miss Amity announced, threatening the sailors with her various weapons pointed straight at their chests.

'Yo! Ho! Ho!' shrieked Little Lew, who was far more dangerous than Miss Amity, and seemed all ready to cut off a dozen heads if the cutlass that he carried had not been a little too heavy for him.

Taking absolutely no notice of Jeffy's scoldings, pleadings and protests, the pair of them drove the terrified sailors back inside the kitchen galley and turned the lock upon them, before racing up to the passenger deck and threatening to blow all the passengers' heads off if they did not hand over all their money and their jewellery and keep quiet.

With the passengers subdued and under lock and key Miss Amity and Little Lew lost no time in charging into the Captain's cabin, seizing the key and making him a prisoner with no explanations at all. The poor man was so taken by surprise that he was locked up before he knew it, while Miss Amity and Little Lew took charge of the ship, with Miss Amity standing at the wheel, and Little Lew singing a sea shanty at the top of his voice.

When Jeffy saw that all his protests were in vain, and that nothing he could say had the slightest effect upon them, neither persuasion nor threats, nor reminding them of all they had once meant to each other, he did the only possible thing that was left for him to do. He flew down to the deck below and released, first the crew from the galley, and then all the passengers from the saloon.

They were not long making the most of their freedom.

Up on the bridge the two hijackers were triumphantly steering the ship back towards England when all of a sudden a stream of cold water hit them between the shoulder blades . . . so sudden and so violent that the wheel was jerked out of Miss Amity's hands and Little Lew jumped six feet into the air. He lost his cutlass and sprang for safety, clutching at the wheel, from which he hung like a small piece of wet washing, yowling sadly to Jeffy for aid.

From the deck below sailors and passengers were handling fire hoses with such deadly aim that in a question of seconds the two hijackers were brought to their knees, and immediately overpowered. A few minutes later, now tied up securely, they were marched in front of the Captain, who, having been rescued from his cabin, and with his ship once more travelling in the right direction under his control, sat ready to administer justice upon the criminals. Jeffy was hiding miserably in a corner of the deck.

Miss Amity readily admitted her guilt. She asked the Captain's pardon with every sign of real regret for her wickedness. She had only done it for excitement, she explained; it had been so terribly boring shut up day after day down there in the hold.

'I thought of it first,' piped up Little Lew. 'And I found the guns, the knives and the swords and things, in people's luggage. I didn't take anything else, and I only borrowed them for fun, I meant to put them back. Jeffy told me always to put things back. Jeffy told me never to take anything that doesn't belong to me, not once, not ever! Always be honest, Jeffy said. And we were going to be quite honest again, after we'd hijacked the ship! Just as Jeffy told us to!'

'And who is Jeffy?' demanded the Captain.

Little Lew pointed a paw towards the wretched

figure of Jeffy crouching in the shadows. 'He's our best friend,' he said proudly.

'It was nothing at all to do with Jeffy,' Miss Amity cried indignantly. 'He is the best, and most honest, the most faithful and loyal friend in all the world! He came right across the sea to find us. And all we have done is to plunge him into disgrace. Oh Jeffy, Jeffy, how could we treat you so? How could we?'

'So this is the cat who said the Bishop would give him a good character!' the Captain said in a rage. 'A criminal cat! A friend of hijackers! I congratulate you, Bishop's cat, on your law-breaking friends!'

'No! No!' shrieked Miss Amity. 'He is good, good, *good*! If we had only done as he advised none of this would have happened. Don't misjudge Jeffy, Captain. Do believe me! He is the best friend that anyone ever had in the whole world!'

The Captain turned his back on her pleading. He gave some brief orders, and Miss Amity and Little Lew were lowered into a small boat and cast away towards a cluster of desert islands, whose palm trees were beginning to feather the distant horizon.

Jeffy made desperate attempts to go with them, but the sailors would not allow it. They remembered that Jeffy had liberated them from the galley and then had freed all the passengers. They thought that Miss Amity and Little Lew were altogether wicked, and did not deserve a cat like him. The Captain was inclined to agree with them.

'You had better go back to your Bishop,' he advised Jeffy, 'if he really exists. You can stay on board until the cruise is over. And the cook had better fatten you up a bit, you have got quite thin and wretched-looking lately. I suppose you have been giving all your rations to your rascally friends.'

At first Jeffy had it in mind to jump overboard and swim after Miss Amity and Little Lew, but one of the sailors held him fast as if he guessed what was in his mind. Gazing over the sailor's shoulder Jeffy saw the little boat grow smaller and smaller in the distance, till it became a nothing-at-all in the wide expanse of sea. Even then the sailors would not let him go free but popped him into the hold and closed the hatch upon him.

Presently they brought him a delicious plate of food and some cream, but now Jeffy had no appetite for eating. He spent his time clearing up the disgraceful muddle that his friends had made of the baggage in their search for arms. Having replaced the cases as best he could, he crept back into the cabin trunk that had so recently held his dear Miss Amity, coiled himself into a corner that still smelt faintly of lavender water, and cried himself to sleep.

16

A Cruise with the Bishop

For the remainder of the cruise Jeffy was well fed and petted, but he was not released from the hold until the ship had berthed in a tropical port, had turned about, and was heading for home.

When at last he was allowed on deck the island breezes were astern of them, and cloudy skies, rain showers and cooler mornings told him that England was not far away.

They berthed at last, and many weeks after he had left the cathedral close Jeffy returned there, jaded, disconsolate, and deeply depressed by the failure of his mission. He felt he ought to have been able to keep Miss Amity under better control.

The Bishop was disappointed too. He had so much looked forward to making Miss Amity's acquaintance, and wished he had been on board himself to persuade her into better behaviour. He comforted Jeffy as best he could.

'Perhaps it is better this way!' he told him, secretly looking forward to a long, quiet winter reunited with his cat, but Jeffy could not be consoled.

'And now I shall never, never see them again!' he mourned.

He was so inconsolable that the Bishop promised to save up his money to go for a cruise among the tropical islands, as soon as he could afford it, in the spring. Even Jeffy realised that the world was such an enormous place they were very unlikely to discover Miss Amity during the short period of a spring cruise, but he was grateful to the Bishop, and it gave him something to think about during the long, dark evenings. He soon had quite a thick pile of travel brochures to sleep upon.

Jeffy did not want to travel on the same ship as before. It had too many unhappy associations. Besides, it was rather expensive. And it only stopped at two ports, while Jeffy and the Bishop intended to visit as many places as possible, even if it meant travelling on a cheap and shabby little boat and being quite uncomfortable.

Secretly, the Bishop and Jeffy hoped that Miss Amity and Little Lew might find their way home again before winter was over. How, Jeffy could not imagine, but he went on hoping. He shuddered to think that they might try to stow away on another boat, but then he remembered that Miss Amity never tried anything twice.

They had their own little boat, of course, in which they had been cast away. But Jeffy had heard the sailors say it was a leaky little craft and would not last five minutes in a storm. From the bottom of his heart Jeffy hoped that they had not attempted to return home in it, but were safe and well, if marooned, on some far-off island under waving palm trees and a tropical sky. (But on which island?) Little Lew would enjoy the fishing.

Winter came to an end. Daffodils blossomed in the cathedral close and in the Bishop's garden. The Bishop went to the travel agency and bought tickets for the cruise he and Jeffy had selected out of all the cruises advertised in the travel catalogues.

The boat was small and it carried only a few passengers.

When the Bishop and Jeffy went on board they found there was nobody else except themselves and the crew. This was because most people wanted to go to famous and fashionable places, but the captain was going to potter about among the tropical islands, trading a little, and this was just the kind of cruise that suited Jeffy and the Bishop best. The cargo they were carrying consisted mostly of books, destined for outlying places, and this too pleased the Bishop, who did not find the voyage a day too long. He read endlessly, while Jeffy sat looking out to sea, sadly wondering whether their homeward journey would find them full of joy, or of disappointment. The Bishop had brought enough money with him to pay for a homeward ticket for Miss Amity if they found her. He was a kind and generous man.

With their hopes and expectations raised high by the voyage, Jeffy and the Bishop approached the tropics, revelling in the beauty of the scenery around them, the shining beaches, bordered by bushes of coloured flowers, all reflected in still lagoons as quiet as looking glasses. They laughed at little native swimming children, offering them pennies to answer questions that never, never brought the answers they were looking for.

The Bishop was tireless in his enquiries. It might have been his own relations that he was seeking, and really it was not difficult to describe a neat little old lady dressed in black, with a black hat and gloves, and a small black cat at her heels, the two of them quite inseparable, and probably washed ashore in a small, leaky rowing boat.

But nobody had seen or heard anything of them. From island to island they cruised, each time with new hopes and expectations, but each time they came away with hopes dashed, quite convinced that Miss Amity and Little Lew had not been seen or heard of.

The twenty days of their cruise were slipping away, and their Captain had nearly visited all the islands on his itinerary. 'After the next port of call we must turn for home,' he told the Bishop, 'but I have still to take a parcel of books to a very remote place at the end of this chain of islands. It is so remote that they keep the prison there so that the prisoners cannot escape from it. But twice a year I take books to the prison library, and these I have with me now.'

'Can one visit the prison?' the Bishop asked, putting into words the question Jeffy longed to ask. At the same time he felt disloyal in even thinking of it. What had an island prison to do with Miss Amity and

Little Lew? But he could not stop thinking about it, and he told the Bishop that he would like to visit the prison very much indeed. The Bishop was too kind and polite to agree that there might be a reason for taking an interest in it, but he repeated his question to the Captain, and said he thought it might be a very interesting place to visit, in a general kind of way.

The Captain shook his head doubtfully. 'I don't think they receive visitors,' he said. 'I have never been inside it myself, not in all these years. I just hand in the books at the entrance, and sign for them. But I don't mind trying for you, not if you really want to have a look at the place. I'll ask when I deliver the books.'

Before they reached the island jetty the prison could plainly be seen standing upon the shore. It was solidly built on the furthest point of the island, where the lagoon gave place to a shark-infested sea. Guards walked up and down on the parapet, looking down on the sharks.

Jeffy's heart sank. If by some dreadful and unfortunate chance his dear Miss Amity and Little Lew had managed to get themselves shut up inside it looked as if only the end of their sentence could possibly free them from such a place.

Once landed at the jetty from the rowing dinghy the Captain had used to bring them ashore, the Bishop and Jeffy sat down in the shade of a palm tree, while the Captain staggered along the sands carrying a load of detective stories towards the prison. He disappeared inside the outer gates.

When he returned they could see from his face that their request was not going to be granted.

'Nobody is allowed inside . . . nobody!' he announced when he reached them. 'There have been too many attempts by the prisoners to escape. The Governor dare not risk it. I am very sorry, Bishop. I did my best.'

'But have people really escaped from this place?' asked the Bishop, incredulously.

'Not actually escaped . . .' said the Captain. 'They try, of course, but in the end they find it better to behave themselves and to be released on parole. I believe there is quite a community of ex-prisoners living in family style on the far side of the island, but you will hardly have time to visit them, because we must leave the island sharply at five o'clock this evening.'

'I would much rather visit the prison itself,' said the Bishop, sensing Jeffy's distress, 'but I'm afraid it seems to be quite out of the question!'

'Couldn't we pretend to be prisoners too?' Jeffy suggested. 'Couldn't the Captain tie us up in handcuffs and hand us over to the guards? Then we would get in without any fuss at all!'

The Bishop was as anxious as Jeffy to leave no stone unturned, and when the Captain agreed that such a plan might be successful he allowed himself to be

bound and shackled for the first time in his long and respectable career. Jeffy's front paws were tied together with the Bishop's watch chain, and his hind legs were shackled with string. They both looked very peculiar indeed, but there was nothing they could do but look at each other and laugh at the picture they presented.

The Captain took a length of rope from the boat and tied it round the Bishop's waist. He led Jeffy by a piece of twine.

Then they set out in a drab little procession for the prison gates.

17

In the Island Prison

Both Jeffy and the Bishop shivered when they arrived at the great guarded gate of the fortress, under the eyes of two armed guards and a warder, who peered at them from behind a grille.

Jeffy and the Bishop fully expected to be challenged as the Captain led them through the entrance to the prison courtyard, and came to a standstill before the grille. But to their surprise the warder greeted them quite naturally, and told the guards to open up the gate.

'Brought 'em with you, did you, Captain?' he said cheerfully. 'Oh well! You'll be glad to get rid of them, I expect! Just hand them over inside and drop in for a cup of tea on your way back. Tell me what's happening in the Cup Tie over there in England!'

As the great steel gates swung open in front of them, Jeffy and the Bishop realised that they had made no plans for leaving the prison, only for getting inside it. The Captain stopped short, and was about to say something when another couple of warders strode up and took charge of his supposed prisoners, jerking the strings out of his hands, while the first pair hustled the Captain into the warder's office. He was still waving his hands in the air and trying to explain when Jeffy and the Bishop were led away into the depths of the fortress, both wondering in some anxiety what they had let themselves in for.

Jeffy's spirits, which had been at their lowest, were suddenly raised to the heights when one of the guards leading him gave a little twitch to the string and remarked cheerfully:

'Well, puddykins! *You* won't be lonely at any rate! We've got another puddykins in here!' Hope rose like a flame inside him.

Jeffy and the Bishop were led through a series of locked doors to a large, central courtyard, completely filled with prisoners. Here, their shackles were removed and they were pushed in to fend for themselves as best they might.

The place was almost like a large camp. Men and women sat with their backs against the walls, or cooked for themselves on charcoal stoves. Hundreds of eyes turned to stare at Jeffy and the Bishop, and then turned again towards whatever they were doing. There seemed to be no end to the eyes, nor to the people. Perhaps after all it was more like a market-place than a camp.

Jeffy and the Bishop stood just where they had been left . . . staring, staring at the faces and the crowded ranks of prisoners. It seemed a far more remote and alien place than any of the islands through which they had been steaming. They had not seen so many people crowded so closely together since they had left home.

Bewildered at first, Jeffy pulled himself together

and began to search purposefully from face to face. It was then that he realised that the Bishop would not recognise Miss Amity if he saw her. They had never met before. It was all very well to describe a little old lady in black, walking down a street, but quite another thing to pick her out of a crowded prison among hundreds of others, some of them dressed in much the same style as herself. The courage and generosity of the Bishop in coming with him to such a place went straight to Jeffy's heart. He was determined to get him out of this situation as quickly as possible.

But first he must finish what he had come to do, and with his heart still beating with hope Jeffy began to search the prisoners' faces one by one.

He soon found this would be an impossible task from where he was standing, so he persuaded the Bishop to sit down on a block of wood, while he trotted off among the prisoners, promising to return as soon as he could.

'Remember, the boat leaves at five o'clock!' the Bishop called after him, betraying for the first time a little nervousness, but Jeffy reassured him, and launched himself into the crowds.

He trotted here and there, from one group to another. A short, black figure wrapped in a shawl set him bounding hopefully towards it, only to find it was not Miss Amity at all. A dozen times his hopes were raised and dashed again. Above the clamour of conversation, the shouts and yells of people arguing and disputing, he kept his ears cocked to catch the first glad cry of: 'Jeffy! Oh, Jeffy!' But it did not come. For it was not easy among so many to see the anxious figure of a searching cat, hunting amongst all the legs and arms, the washing hung from pegs on the walls, the cooking pots and braziers, the water jars and wooden stools. Jeffy was submerged in it all. Like a wraith or a shadow he quartered the prison yard almost unnoticed, but always hopeful . . . if Miss Amity and Little Lew were here he was going to find them!

And then, suddenly, just as he reached the very furthest boundary of the prison courtyard, something small perched high up on the wall caught his eye for the shortest possible second before it vanished. Something black and swift and thin. A cat!

Jeffy sped to the foot of the wall and craned upwards. He raised himself on his hind legs and stretched as far up the wall as he could reach, calling and calling:

'Lew! Lew! Lew!'

A prisoner sitting on the ground close by reached out and grasped him by the scruff of the neck.

'Hey, pussycat! Here's another of 'em! We can have pussycats for supper!'

'Lew! Lew!' shrieked Jeffy, kicking and struggling.

The prisoner only laughed and held him more tightly.

'He's fatter than the other one!' he told his friends

sitting round him. 'We'll have pussycat pie!'

Jeffy scratched and bit and struggled. The prisoner jeered at him, holding him so tight that he was almost strangled. The man sitting next to him drew out a long, thin, sharp and shining knife. Jeffy thought his last moment had come.

'Lew!' he panted with his last breath. 'Lew!'

There came a flying black shadow from the top of the wall above his head. Like a small hawk swooping on its prey the shadow plummeted out of the air straight on to the top of the prisoner's head, all claws stretched, clutching at hair and flesh. The man roared aloud and dropped Jeffy. The prisoner with the knife leapt backwards in a fright, loosing his weapon, and Jeffy fled for his life through the legs of the milling crowds, while his rescuer returned to his watchpost on the wall, well out of reach of the prisoners below. It was a small, black, slim cat, but it was not Little Lew.

Jeffy arrived panting at the Bishop's side. The old man was becoming very restive, and anxiously watching for his return. They were wondering what to do next when with a jangling of keys the great door behind them opened, and the Governor of the fortress appeared on the threshold with the Captain at his side, still doing his best to explain his story.

'The guards just whisked them away from under my nose, Governor, before I could say a thing, sir!' the Captain was explaining. 'I just stopped to say a word to my friend at the gate, and *whoosh!* they were gone! Never gave me a chance, sir! Two of my passengers, sir, their return passages fully paid! And one of them a Bishop!'

The Governor hastened to the Bishop's side.

'My lord! My lord! My deepest and most contrite apologies!' he exclaimed. 'I cannot begin to voice my regrets for such a stupid blunder! I trust you have not been subjected to any unpleasantness, my lord? The unfortunate affair has only just come to my ears! And your cat, my lord! Has he been threatened or assaulted? There is a ruffianly cat among the convicts here . . . has your reverend moggins come to any harm?'

'Not in the least! Not at all!' said the Bishop happily. 'Nobody took the least notice of me personally, I am glad to say. And I believe your convict cat was able to save my Jeffy from a very embarrassing situation.'

'I am so thankful, so thankful!' said the Governor, leading the Bishop and Jeffy back through the corridors to the welcome freedom of the outer gate. 'I will see that his parole is advanced by several weeks.'

The Bishop, the Captain and Jeffy gratefully refused the cup of tea that the Governor would have pressed upon them. It would soon be dark, the Captain explained, and he was anxious to navigate the rather tricky channel between the islands before the sun went down.

Hastily making their farewells the Bishop and Jeffy left the fortress, and then remembered that they had not asked the Governor for any possible news of Miss Amity and Little Lew. At the moment their feelings were very mixed – thankfulness that they had escaped from a rather nasty predicament and deep disappointment that their last opportunity had vanished, and after all their voyaging and searching they had to return home confessing themselves beaten.

They walked back very quietly towards the boat.

18

Sunset on the Island

The setting sun shed an unearthly beauty over the island, painting the silent sands with an exquisite shade of apricot. The Captain's little rowing boat, that would take them out to deeper water where the steamer lay at anchor, huddled close to the jetty, scarcely moving in the small, quiet waves.

They walked silently along the jetty in procession, first the Captain, then the Bishop, and lastly Jeffy, who cast many mournful glances over his shoulder, as if even at this very last moment Miss Amity might appear between the palm trees, or Little Lew signal to him from the edges of the forest beyond.

Neither of them did, but just as Jeffy was on the point of leaping lightly onto the dinghy after the Bishop, he saw something on the sand, by the edge of the lagoon, that made him jump backwards instead, and remain petrified, staring at the sands below as if he had been turned into stone.

'Come, Jeffy, come!' said the Bishop impatiently. He was only too anxious to leave the island now, and the Captain was already unknotting the rope that moored them to the jetty.

But Jeffy continued to stare at the sands beside the lagoon, and the Bishop could not imagine what he was staring at. The sun was dipping rapidly towards the horizon and the Captain could not conceal his impatience to be rejoining his ship.

'Jeffy!' the Bishop commanded sternly, but instead of obeying him, Jeffy jumped off the side of the jetty on to the sand, put his nose to the ground and began to sniff again at the something he had discovered there.

Could it be a fish he had found, the Bishop wondered, clambering back on to the jetty in spite of the Captain's protests. He meant to pick up Jeffy and carry him aboard. But first he wanted to see what was engaging his attention. Jeffy was following it now, moving along as if on a trail, away from the dinghy, away from the jetty.

'JEFFY!' the Bishop roared.

He was on the sands himself now, peering for the starfish, the crab, or whatever it was that made Jeffy so stubborn and obstinate, but all that he could see were footprints, the usual footprints one might see on the sand around any jetty anywhere . . . but . . . .

One set of footprints, neat and small, led away from the sea, and beside them ran a smaller set, even neater, and quite round and even. They were very much like Jeffy's own footprints.

They ran along the sands by the edge of the lagoon, and Jeffy was now following on the trail of them, where they turned away from the sea towards the forest.

The Bishop cried: 'Jeffy! Jeffy! Those are our own footprints . . . don't you see?'

But Jeffy took no notice, and all of a sudden the

Bishop realised that the footprints they had made themselves were not on this side of the jetty at all, but on the other. And they were heading in the opposite direction. Tentatively he fitted his shoe into one of the prints and found that he entirely blotted it out. The print was much more like the footprint of a lady.

The Captain was shouting to them now. He couldn't wait any longer, he said, they must come at once before the sun went down.

'Jeffy! We must go!' the Bishop urged him.

For one moment Jeffy stopped and looked back at him.

All the love and devotion and gratitude for the last few years shone in his eyes as he looked into the face of his friend. But behind it shone another, older devotion, steeped in such utter loyalty and faithfulness that the Bishop almost quailed.

Then Jeffy turned back to his quest, and with his nose low to the ground like a dog, he bounded up the shore into the palm trees, putting more distance between them with every bound, until he vanished into the shadows of the forest.

The Bishop stood dumbfounded as Jeffy disappeared, swallowed up by the trees. Slowly he returned to the jetty, where the Captain had already cast off the boat, but was still waiting with it at the water's edge.

'It's now or never, Bishop!' he cried as the Bishop drew near. 'We'll never get through those reefs in the dark, and my company fines me for every day I'm overdue. Come on board, sir! Never mind about the old cat! I guess he doesn't care about the sea!'

The Bishop made a little pushing gesture as though casting off the dinghy from the shore. He turned away, waving a salute to the Captain over his shoulder.

'Aren't you coming, sir?' the Captain shouted, just one time more.

The Bishop gave a weary shake of his head and began to trudge up the sand in the direction in which Jeffy had disappeared. Hardly believing what had happened, the Captain picked up his oars and rowed back towards his ship.

'Barmy!' he muttered, watching the Bishop slowly trudging out of sight. 'Plain barmy! I might as well have left him in the prison after all!'

He was still shaking his head when he came aboard, and steered his cargo boat by the sun's last rays through the tortuous reefs and shallows of the island chain, on its course for home.

Darkness fell with tropical suddenness, and the Bishop began to realise what he had done. Not only had he thrown away the chance of his homeward voyage (his tickets and money were still in his cabin), but he could not think how he would ever get home at all, and worst of all he had lost Jeffy too.

The evening shadows closed in about him, and the forest was wrapped in a deep purple velvet cloak of night, that fell so suddenly and silently around him that everything that a moment ago had been living and growing and blossoming seemed to have been swallowed up in an inky gulf.

The Bishop was not a fearful man, but he was overwhelmed by the great unknown stretching all about him. Standing with his back against a palm tree he prayed to be shown what to do, and as he prayed a long, lonely wail of anguish rose on the night air from the depth of the forest.

'Jeffy!' called the Bishop. 'Jeffy! Jeffy!'

There came a far-off shivering of the wind in the leaves that grew louder, like a stream of water dashing through foliage. Then something burst through the undergrowth, something vibrating and trembling that flung itself wildly at the Bishop's feet and knees, butting with its head against his ankles.

'Oh, Bishop! Oh dear, dear Bishop!' Jeffy panted, almost beside himself with joy. 'I thought you had gone, and I was all alone!'

The Bishop and Jeffy slept under the palm tree all through the tropical night, and in the morning they resumed their quest. The footprints were lost in the undergrowth, but Jeffy's nose led them as surely as any hound along the trail. Sometimes he went back to pick up the scent he had lost, sometimes he hurried ahead where it seemed strong and certain. A tuft of black hair on a twig set them laughing for joy. It could only belong to Little Lew, though the scent was nearly gone from it, and Jeffy thought he had passed this way some time ago . . . even months.

Their progress was very slow. They seemed to be passing through the very centre of the island, and when darkness fell again there was no change in the forest that hemmed them in on either side.

The trail had grown faint, and as they settled down for a second night under the stars the Bishop could not help thinking wistfully of his home in the close beside the cathedral, and his comfortable cabin in the cargo boat, heading now for England without him. But he was inspired by Jeffy's loyalty and faithfulness, and did not betray his feelings as they huddled close together in the dark.

In the morning they went on, eating fruit and berries, and becoming more and more footsore and torn by the undergrowth, but towards midday Jeffy stopped suddenly and said: 'I can smell smoke! We are coming to *people*!'

The Bishop could not smell anything, but Jeffy's words made him feel much more cheerful. It had been a long and dreary journey, and he longed for some signs of human habitation.

The trees thinned out . . . blue sky glinted above and before them. The forest ran out into a wide and sandy bay, on the outskirts of which was spread an unmistakable village, busy with people of every kind and colour. And where the forest met the sand the same double line of footsteps ran out before them, straight into the heart of the village, where they became swallowed up in hundreds more, but all so obviously barefooted that even here the neat toes and heels showed up quite distinctly.

There were all kinds of people in the settlement: old, young, black, white, yellow, pinkish, darkish, bearded, clean-shaven, men and women, boys, girls and babies. And they were all busy over the common and everyday tasks of running their homes in a village – washing, sweeping, weaving, fishing, building, baking, making ropes, making boats, making clothes, even making shoes, though very few people seemed to wear them.

As the Bishop and Jeffy approached them they were welcomed with interest, and always the same question:

'Are you parolers?'

'Are we what?' asked the Bishop, puzzled.

'Parolers! On parole . . . out of the prison there!' the people said, amused by the Bishop's ignorance.

'No, we're not parolers,' the Bishop said. He added: 'Just visitors.'

'We're all parolers here,' one of the villagers said cheerfully, peeling a mountain of potatoes. 'You know . . . set free to be good! Don't you know what a paroler is, Mister?'

'Well yes, I do,' said the Bishop. 'Do you mean to tell me every one of you has been in prison?'

'Every one!' said the villager, not without a certain

pride. 'That's why we're here, Mister!'

'And what happens to you afterwards, when you have worked out your parole?' the Bishop asked curiously.

'Ah! Then we go home,' said the ex-prisoner. 'But it's not as easy as that. We have to go through the school first, and if Miss Amity doesn't think we're ready we have to do some more parole. But if she says we're all right for ever and ever then, that's it, and we're off!'

'Miss Amity!' exclaimed the Bishop and Jeffy together, almost fainting in their excitement.

'She's over there in the school,' the ex-prisoner indicated. 'Behind the Infant School. That's the one in front. That's where they teach the babies not to be bad. Lew sees to it.'

'Lew!' murmured the Bishop and Jeffy in the same breath.

With trembling footsteps they crossed the village to an open space between the trees where the notice INFANT SCHOOL was slung between two palms. From afar they could see the rows of small benches crowded with children, and hear the pattern of their lessons repeated on the air. And as they approached, the words of the lesson became clearer. The children were chanting over and over again:

'Always be clean and tidy!
Always be honest!
Never take what doesn't belong to you!
Not once! NOT EVER!

Think before you act and wash before you think!'
They began all over again.

Jeffy and the Bishop saw the children eagerly repeating their lesson, with their eyes fixed on Little Lew, who marched up and down in front of the class, his fur spruce and tidy, his tail brushed and clean, carefully watching to see that every pupil was paying attention to what it was saying and acting accordingly. He was conducting the rhythm with a little cane.

Suddenly catching sight of the unexpected visitors, Little Lew dropped the cane, stopped for one minute on his hind legs with his mouth wide open, and then took the three last benches in a bound, as he flung himself at Jeffy's feet.

'Oh Jeffy! Oh Jeffy! Jeffy! Jeffy! I thought I'd never see you again! Oh dear, good Jeffy, you don't know how I did miss you! How ashamed I was at being so bad and wicked! I meant all the rest of my life to be good like you! Missammitty and me got to this island in our little boat, and now I'm making other people good too. I keep telling them how good you were and how bad I was, and how they've got to grow up just like you, though I was so bad I'd lost the chance of ever seeing you again. I've got baddies too, Jeffy, but I'm teaching them to be good. Look!' He pointed with an eager paw to a bench set apart, where a dozen little children sat weeping, and surveying their bright green fingers that seemed to have been dipped in some kind of indelible dye.

'What do you say . . . over there?' Little Lew shouted severely, and the woebegone chorus chanted:

'Jeffy wouldn't like it!
Jeffy wouldn't like it!'

and then retreated into their tears.

'They've been pinching things,' Little Lew remarked with satisfaction. 'But they won't do it again. Nobody likes going about with green fingers. They get laughed at.'

'Who is your mister?' he asked Jeffy in a loud whisper. Jeffy hastily introduced the Bishop.

'Welcome to my school, my lord!' said Little Lew puffing himself out. 'We are very honoured to receive a Bishop on parole!'

'*Not* on parole!' Jeffy interrupted earnestly. 'And Lew, where . . . *where* is Missammitty?'

'There!' said Little Lew, pointing to a large hut behind the Infant School. 'She does the grown-ups, but the little ones are more important. Prevention is better than cure, isn't it, Bishop? Oh I must tell her Jeffy is here! I must! I must!' he shrieked leaping high in the air in his excitement. 'Here you, class! Begin on the next one, and go on and on till I come back!'

Little Lew galloped across the sand to the school hut, followed more sedately by the Bishop and Jeffy, though they were very nearly as excited as Lew was. Behind them, the shrill chorus of baby voices took up the refrain:

'Who's good?

Jeffy Cat!
Who's honest?
Jeffy Cat!
Who's kind and faithful?
Jeffy! Jeffy! Jeffy!'

Jeffy felt so overcome with bashfulness that he hid behind the Bishop without raising his eyes from the ground, so the first thing he saw was Miss Amity's little black boots as she rushed out of the hut to meet him and gather him to her heart.

It was the happiest possible reunion.

The Bishop's eyes filled with tears as he watched the meeting between the elderly little lady and her cat. All past misdemeanours and misdoings seemed to fall off her shoulders as grateful tears rolled down her cheeks on to Jeffy's coat. Anyone at this minute who saw her trotting down the High Street might have thought her indescribably shabby and careworn, but to Jeffy she shone with a light of pure goodness that he had never seen her wear before. His dear Miss Amity had worked out her parole. She was being good for ever and ever.

He rejoiced in introducing her to the Bishop, while in her turn Miss Amity showed off her school with the greatest enthusiasm. All the trades and industries carried out in the village began here. Every person found out what best he could do, and did it to the best of his or her ability. So far as Jeffy could see, there was no bench of green hands in Miss Amity's school, only a lot of busy ones.

'Many of them are quite ready to go back to their homes,' Miss Amity told them. 'And I *know* they will never be criminals again. In three months' time a steamer will come to the island, and all those who are fit will leave us.'

Jeffy and the Bishop were delighted to hear this. It meant that they would not be marooned for ever on this island. Only a few more weeks to wait and they would be able to take Miss Amity, and Little Lew of course, back to the peace and quiet of the cathedral close, to live happily ever after.

The Bishop helped Miss Amity to run the school, and he taught the ex-prisoners about God. This helped them to be good too. He wished there had been more time while he was on the island to build a cathedral, as they would all have enjoyed it so much.

Jeffy helped Little Lew in the Infant School, and was adored by all the little children. Nobody had any more green hands because they knew that if they had they would not be able to stroke Jeffy. Little Lew made Jeffy be headmaster and went into one of the classes himself. He said he had such an awful lot to learn that only Jeffy could teach him. Jeffy was very touched. He changed the Jeffy songs into Washing Songs, and the Bishop taught them children's hymns and choruses.

But Little Lew had only to whisper: 'Jeffy wouldn't like it!' and everybody was instantly as good as gold.

As the day approached for the steamer to arrive, the ex-prisoners who were leaving began to pack up their possessions and talk with great excitement about their homes. The Bishop began to talk to Miss Amity about his too, but oddly enough it was with less and less enthusiasm. And Jeffy found he had to force himself to purr with pleasure when the Bishop described the cosy parlour on winter nights, with the fire crackling in the grate, and the carol singers carolling outside, while the great cathedral clock struck nine. He and Little Lew would be curled up before the blaze, and Miss Amity and the Bishop would be drinking a cup of tea together, Miss Amity having come over to visit from the cottage the Bishop was going to find her to live in, in the cathedral close.

But would she be bored? Would Little Lew be bored? What would they find to do with themselves from dawn to dark, after the busy life they had been leading on the island? Would they turn again to crime just to keep themselves occupied? Jeffy shivered at the thought. He even dreamed about it at night, and he noticed that the Bishop too became quiet and pensive, talking less and less about the joys of home.

And then Jeffy found Little Lew howling on the shore.

'Whatever is the matter?' Jeffy asked in alarm.

'I don't want to go,' Little Lew wept. 'I don't want to leave the little children. I know they'll all grow up bad if I do! But I don't want to leave Missammitty either! And I don't want to leave Mister Bishop! And I don't want to leave the island! I don't want to leave *you*, Jeffy! I don't want to leave anybody! I want to stay with everybody for ever and ever!'

Jeffy rushed away in distress to find the Bishop and Miss Amity, only to find them just as unsettled as Little Lew. Miss Amity was wretched at leaving her school, but was miserable at the thought of the Bishop going home alone. And the Bishop did not want to leave Miss Amity. Working together on the island a respect had grown up between them that had turned to affection, and none of the four of them could now bear to think of life without each other.

Finding the Bishop so depressed, and Miss Amity so restless, and Little Lew so hysterical, Jeffy took matters into his own hands.

'Why don't you marry Miss Amity and we'll all stay here?' he said to the Bishop.

'Oh Jeffy, what a wonderful idea!' said the Bishop, brightening up immediately. 'But do you think she would ever accept me?'

Jeffy went to Miss Amity, who was grieving behind the schoolhouse.

'Why don't you and the Bishop get married and not leave the island at all?' he asked her. Miss Amity's face shone with delight.

'But do you think he would ever ask me?' she said with awe.

'I'm sure of it!' said Jeffy, and he flew back to the

Bishop to tell him the happy news: 'Yes, she will!'

'But what about you, Jeffy?' they asked him a little later, when everything had been decided except for that very important point. 'We might have thought of it before, by ourselves, only we didn't think you would want to stay on the island for ever, like us.'

Jeffy's only desire was to live beside the people he loved for the rest of his days, and with the Bishop to look after Miss Amity and be responsible for her, he felt that his worries were behind him at last.

A chaplain came over from the prison to marry Miss Amity and the Bishop, and before the ex-prisoners left the island there was a splendid wedding in the village, followed by a party that nobody would ever forget.

The steamer left at last, and the Bishop, Miss Amity, Little Lew and Jeffy were left behind. In the weeks that followed more ex-prisoners on parole came to the village from the fortress, and between them the Bishop, Miss Amity, Jeffy and Little Lew turned them into honest citizens.

The Bishop built a spendid cathedral on the island.

It was bigger than the prison, and survived long after the prison went out of use and was pulled down.

It survived long after Jeffy had at last lived out his nine lives, but he was never forgotten. In one of the stained glass windows, facing out to sea, was a portrait of Jeffy, painted by a very clever ex-prisoner. Inside the cathedral too, the stained glass cat looked down on the little children saying their prayers, and reminded them to behave themselves.

Outside, the setting sun twinkled on the window, and outlined the cat in a blaze of light.

Then, little boys and girls kicking their heels on the shore, or setting off to get into mischief through sheer idleness or lack of something better to do, caught the glance of Jeffy's eyes upon them, and whispered: *'Jeffy wouldn't like it!'*

And they scuttled off in the opposite direction, determined after all to be good.